WARWICK'S VILLAGES

Glimpses FROM THE PAST

DONALD A. D'AMATO

Charleston London

Published by The History Press
Charleston, SC 29403
www.historypress.net

Images are courtesy of the author unless otherwise noted.

First published 2009

Manufactured in the United States

ISBN 978.1.59629.599.5

Library of Congress Cataloging-in-Publication Data

D'Amato, Donald A., 1931-
Warwick's villages : glimpses from the past / Donald A. D'Amato.
p. cm.
ISBN 978-1-59629-599-5
1. Warwick (R.I.)--History. I. Title.
F89.W2D34 2009
974.5'4--dc22

2008053142

Notice: The information in this book is true and complete to the best of our knowledge. It is offered without guarantee on the part of the author or The History Press. The author and The History Press disclaim all liability in connection with the use of this book.

Contents

FOREWORD

As a lifelong Warwick resident whose family history here dates back more than 150 years, I am honored to write the foreword for my friend Don D'Amato's latest work.

Since our humble beginning as the settlement of Shawomet more than 360 years ago, Warwick residents have embodied the spirit of community, compassion for others and an honest and effective government. In the centuries since our founding, we have retained the close-knit feel of a much smaller community, even though Warwick has grown into Rhode Island's second-largest city, with nearly ninety thousand residents.

The city of Warwick is actually composed of more than thirty villages, each with its own unique place in history. Don's latest installment spotlights five of these hamlets, which remain vitally important to the fabric of our community: Apponaug, the seat of our municipal government; Conimicut, a shoreline community that's home to the last lighthouse in the nation to be electrified; Hillsgrove, which hosts T.F. Green Airport; Pawtuxet, site of the burning of the HMS *Gaspee*; and Pontiac, a vibrant mill community that was the original location of the Fruit of the Loom company.

As a former history teacher for the Warwick school system and the Community College of Rhode Island, the author of a weekly column in our community newspaper and the city of Warwick's historian, Don has brought Warwick's rich and colorful past to life. On behalf of the countless citizens who have a deeper understanding of, and appreciation for, our heritage because of him, I thank him for his ongoing enthusiasm and dedication to our community.

Foreword

Finally, I applaud all who have gone before us and have worked to make the city of Warwick a vibrant, successful and important part of the state of Rhode Island.

Scott Avedisian
Mayor

APPONAUG

Throughout most of my life, I have had a hate-love relationship with my birthplace. Sometimes I have been proud of it, sometimes ashamed to acknowledge any relation to it…I hope good planning will make my village attractive to visitors and residents and that once again it will become a place with a future.
—*Dorothy Mayor,* I Remember Apponaug

Apponaug, one of the oldest villages in Warwick, is located at a key point on the Old Pequot Path, now Post Road and Route 1. It has been at the center of much activity from the time of the Native Americans to the present. Today, the village has been revitalized and Dorothy Mayor's hopes have materialized.

Nearly two thousand years before Roger Williams established his colony at Providence, the Apponaug section of Warwick was inhabited by members of the Narragansett Indian tribe. Williams first trod the Old Pequot Path (Post Road) through Apponaug on his journey from Providence to the trading post at Cocumscussoc, near present-day Wickford, in 1636. Williams said that the Indians called the place *Oppenenauchack*, which he defined as meaning "oyster."

Excavations by the Narragansett Archaeological Society help provide a picture of life around the cove in the prehistoric period. In 1954 and 1955, archaeologists worked at an area called Sweet's Meadows. In a very well-documented report written by the late William Fowler, we learn that the Indians encamped "on the northerly side of the town of Apponaug…along a small spring-fed brook, which empties into Apponaug Cove." He surmises that "the brook, together with other advantages, must have made this

Visitors coming up Post Road from East Greenwich are greeted with this handsome sign near the Brayton Cemetery.

location a favorite place over a long span of years." It is estimated that the camp was occupied from approximately 100 BC to AD 1600. In 1685, after King Philip's War had removed the Indians from the area, a man named Sweet came into possession of the property and the sandy meadow became known as Sweet's Meadow. In time, it changed to Sweet-Meadow, the name commonly used today.

In 1642, when Samuel Gorton and his followers came to the area that we today call Warwick, the natives had already abandoned the Sweet-Meadow site. With the exception of the discoveries made by archaeologists during the twentieth century, there are, unfortunately, but few reminders of the long tenure of occupancy by the Indians.

After King Philip's War (1675–76), the Gortonites were able to expand to the west from Conimicut Village and Warwick Neck. The area most in use in the last part of the seventeenth century was the Four-Mile Common, the excellent meadowland between Conimicut Shore and Apponaug Cove. By the turn of the century, the second generation of settlers had moved into much of the land around the cove in the area that the Indians had occupied for many centuries.

Apponaug

The Drum Rock

It was during the late nineteenth century that a great deal of curiosity arose over a number of "Drum Rocks." Speculation on their uses and their value to the Native Americans grew, and interest in the large rock at Apponaug attracted the attention of geologists and local historians. In 1839, an eminent geologist, Charles T. Jackson, wrote the following:

> *In Apponaug, in the township of Warwick, there is a curious mass of rock delicately balanced upon two points, so as to be moved with great ease by the hand, and it is said it's even rocked by the wind...By rocking it a sound is produced audible to a great distance.*

Jackson was informed that the sound could be heard during the stillness of night from a distance of six or eight miles. O.P. Fuller, in his *History of Warwick*, mentions a Drum Rock that was probably used by the Indians "to give alarm in time of danger and to call the people together at their pawwaw gatherings."

Today, the rock, which is located approximately six-tenths of a mile from the Post Road entrance to Cowesett Hills just before Building 16, is silent. In 1984, an attempt was made to enrich Warwick's heritage by getting the rock to "boom" again and by replacing the plaque that once marked the rock. At the time of the ceremony and rededication, John Brown, Narragansett tribal historian on archaeological matters, took exception to the interpretation on the plaque and asserted that the rock was not used by his tribe. He is quoted as saying in August 1984: "Our oral history and oral tradition says nothing about this rock. It has no relevance to us at all."

Almost immediately following Brown's statement, a number of local historians, including the late Dorothy Mayor, defended the concept that the rock was used by the Indians. For much of Warwick's history, the Drum Rock at Apponaug has been an important part of the village's identity. Although not everyone is in agreement over what part the rock played in prehistoric times, no one disputes the fact that the large rock made a deep, booming sound. Dot Mayor, in her recollection of Apponaug during the early part of the twentieth century, recalled playing on Drum Rock: "Drum Rock was so much a part of my life...it was so distinctive a landmark. It was private land and there were only cows around it." She recalled that the rock was not easy to move and "it took four or five little kids to rock it."

Today, the stone is again marked with a plaque as it was in the 1930s. The general feeling among the area's historians is that Drum Rock serves

The lure of the Drum Rock is as strong today as it was in the nineteenth century. Little Charley Heinig intuitively headed to it and tried to rock it.

as one of the few reminders that long before Roger Williams and Samuel Gorton came to the Old Pequot Path, there was a thriving Native American community here.

THE EARLY ENGLISH SETTLERS

The first mention of Apponaug in the Warwick town records was on May 27, 1663. At that time, Apponaug Cove was the westernmost point of the area known as the Four-Mile Common. This designation was applied to the land from Greenwich Bay to the northern boundary of the Shawomet Purchase, bounded on the east by the early Gorton village and the west by Apponaug Cove.

The settlement at Apponaug did not take place during the time of the first generation of settlers. Problems with the Massachusetts Bay Colony, a limited population and difficulties with the Indian sachem Pomham and his followers made it impossible to establish a settlement in Apponaug until after King Philip's War (1676). After that dreadful conflict, the power of the Narragansett Indians was broken and Pomham was killed. Significant improvements in living conditions came when an increase in population and greater success in farming and trade made it possible for Warwick to attract skilled laborers. These skilled mechanics were very instrumental in establishing the village at Apponaug.

John Micarter Comes to Apponaug

John Micarter was a skilled laborer who came to the area. Micarter was interested in setting up a "fulling mill" and chose Apponaug as the site for this enterprise. As the second generation of settlers came, they demanded better dwellings and finer clothing. As a result, fulling mills were in great demand in the seventeenth century. "Fulling" is the process of cleansing, scouring and pressing woven woolen goods to make them stronger and firmer. Cloth is put in a trough with "fuller's earth" (usually clay), and the pestles are beat on it to thicken and scour the cloth. After about forty-eight to sixty-five hours of this treatment, the result is considerable shrinkage of the cloth. The threads are firm and close together, and the tendency for the cloth to unravel has been eliminated. Apponaug had soil that contained this "fuller's earth" or clay, which was necessary to separate the grease and oil from the cloth. Realizing this, and finding the area ideal for his enterprise, Micarter asked for and received permission to build a mill at the stream near the cove, and a village was born.

Apparently, not long after the mill was put into operation, Micarter decided to leave and sold his fulling mill to Jeremiah Westcott in 1698. In the spring of 1702, Westcott sold his interest to Samuel Greene. The acquisition of the property by Samuel Greene was a significant event in the village's history, as it was through the leadership of the Greene family that Apponaug developed during the eighteenth and early nineteenth centuries. The Samuel Greene who purchased the mill in 1702 was the son of Major John Greene, one of the most powerful and important figures in early Rhode Island history.

In addition to the property Samuel owned in Apponaug, he also purchased land and a house in Cowesett from his brother-in-law, Samuel Gorton Jr. The house became very famous later as the residence of Governor William Greene Jr. It was a meeting place for many of the Revolutionary leaders in the colony, and Governor William Greene (1778–86) was a strong leader in the latter part of the Revolutionary War. Governor Greene married beautiful Catharine Ray of Block Island, a close friend of Benjamin Franklin. On a number of occasions, Franklin was a guest at this house. Mrs. Greene's niece, Catharine Littlefield, and Major General Nathanael Greene, Rhode Island's most significant Revolutionary War hero, were married in that house in 1774.

Samuel Greene left his Apponaug property to his son, Samuel Greene Jr., who played an important role in operating the fulling mill and in developing the village. Samuel Greene Jr. died in 1780 and left the mill to his son, Caleb (1737–1813). During the Revolutionary War, Caleb was captain of the militia. Sensing the need for other products in Apponaug, he added a gristmill and a sawmill to his enterprises. In conjunction with his cousin Jacob Greene, he entered in trade, and all of his ventures proved profitable during the Revolutionary War and the period following.

While General Nathanael Greene and his cousin Colonel Christopher Greene won great fame as members of the Continental army, Jacob Greene, Nathanael's brother, served in the General Assembly. He, too, played a significant role as he helped to procure much-needed supplies for the Continental army. During the Revolutionary War, Jacob, as the oldest brother, supervised his family's business and operated a store in Apponaug. He and Caleb, who owned the mills in the village, helped bring trade and prosperity to wartime Apponaug.

One astute twentieth-century writer, Ernest L. Lockwood, in his memorable 1937 book, *Episodes in Warwick History*, wrote, "Apponaug Cove was the scene of considerable activity during the period when Jacob Greene & Co. shipped iron forging to ports throughout the country." He added, "Apponaug enjoyed the distinction of having been the center of a good deal of activity in ship building." Sloops and schooners that played an important role in the commerce of the Rhode Island colony were designed and built here. As late as 1800, the cove could accommodate sloops of fifteen tons.

During the period in which Jacob Greene was most active in Apponaug, the village experienced growth in both size and prosperity. It was so dramatic a growth that many villagers felt this was the beginning of a great era for the village. Members of the Greene, Wilbur, Stafford and Arnold families waxed even more prosperous as the early nineteenth century progressed. The degree of success was so exhilarating that one contemporary stated very seriously that "Apponaug will yet be bigger than London."

Part of the reason for Apponaug's growth at this time was the almost constant move westward from Old Warwick. This was hastened during the Revolution, when the British stopped the ferry service between Warwick Neck, Providence and Newport. Apponaug, along Post Road, was an important part of the overland artery that transported goods between Connecticut and Boston. When the war ended and the maritime trade increased, Apponaug Cove enjoyed great prosperity. Once Rhode Islanders began to take part in the China trade and trade increased with

The Greene Memorial House has served Apponaug well over the years and is a fitting tribute to one of its great heroes.

Europe, unprecedented growth and prosperity came to the village and its inhabitants.

For many years, Caleb Greene Jr. had witnessed prosperity, as had his father, Caleb, and his grandfather, Samuel Greene Jr.. Like so many other members of Warwick's early families, Caleb Jr. had taken to the sea to seek his fortune. For many years, this proved a good decision. Unfortunately, the Napoleonic Wars, the Embargo Act and the War of 1812 ended the period of prosperity for much of New England. Eventually, because the restrictions on trade seriously infringed on Greene's profit, he turned to his father's textile mill to provide for his family. In time, this once prosperous mariner found that various plans for his sons' education had to be changed in order to economize.

In 1795, in thriving economic times, Caleb Greene Jr. built the house at 15 Centerville Road, shortly after his marriage to Sarah Robinson. Caleb Greene fathered a large family. In 1801, his second son, George Sears Greene, was born in the Apponaug house. Difficult economic times made it impossible for Caleb to finance his son's education. Fortunately, George Sears Greene, at age eighteen, was appointed to the U.S. Military Academy at West Point. In 1823, he graduated with honors and entered the army as a second lieutenant. During the next twelve years, he served as an officer of artillery and taught mathematics at West Point. While serving in the army, he married Elizabeth Vinton, who bore him three children.

The happiness of G.S. Greene's early years quickly disintegrated as tragedy struck in 1832, when Elizabeth and two of their children died within a seven-month period. Greene, at thirty-one years of age, found the grief almost impossible to bear. His only relief seemed to be in books, and he spent most of his off-duty hours studying law, medicine and civil engineering. By 1835, his outstanding talents enabled him to pass several examinations, which gave him the right to practice both law and medicine.

Greene soon realized that promotions in the peacetime army were very slow and that there was a great demand for civil engineers in the new, exciting and profitable business of railroad construction. In 1836, he resigned from the army and pursued a very successful career as a civil engineer, a profession he practiced for the next twenty-five years. In 1837, he married Martha Dana, and the couple had six children.

THE CIVIL WAR

When the Civil War erupted between the Union and the Confederacy, George Sears Greene was already sixty years old. Fully aware of the desperate need for trained officers and civil engineers, Greene reentered the army and was commissioned colonel of the Sixtieth Regiment, New York Volunteers. In 1862, he was appointed brigadier general. His greatest accomplishment came in the crucial action at the Battle of Gettysburg, where his courage and ability to assess a battlefield situation proved highly important. On July 2, 1863, General Greene's brigade was placed on Culp's Hill, which protected the right flank of the Union army at Cemetery Ridge. General Greene was left with only five regiments to defend the hill. Greene used his engineering and military skills to fortify the hill, and during the night of July 2 and the morning of July 3, his troops were able to withstand the attack of twenty-two Confederate regiments. This proved to be one of the decisive factors in the battle, as it helped the Union army strengthen its artillery on Cemetery Ridge. Had the Confederacy taken Cemetery Ridge, victory could have been theirs.

As a reminder of this heroic action, a boulder taken from Culp's Hill at Gettysburg has been placed in the small Greene Cemetery off Tanner Avenue in Apponaug. A plaque tells of the exploits of George Sears Greene. Because of vandalism, the plaque was removed from the stone and is now in City Hall, where it is more accessible to the general public.

A Military Family

While George Sears Greene was becoming one of Rhode Island's most colorful Civil War generals, two of his sons were also distinguishing themselves on the battlefields. One of them, Samuel Dana Greene, was the executive officer onboard the Union ship *Monitor* and took part in the classic battle with the *Merrimac* in 1862. Another son, Brevet Major Charles T. Greene, was at the Battle of Ringgold, Georgia, where he lost his right leg as a result of a cannon shot. General Greene's youngest son, Major General Francis Vinton Greene, too young for the Civil War, served during the Spanish-American War. Francis Vinton Greene gave the Greene family house of his ancestors to the Rhode Island Episcopal Convention. His intention was to have it used by St. Barnabas Church as a rectory and to have it maintained as a memorial to his illustrious father.

The Greene Memorial House was used by St. Barnabas Church as a rectory, church school and for religious functions from 1900 to 1926. In 1911, a fire broke out in Apponaug and the wooden church that was St. Barnabas burned to the ground. When the present church was built in 1926, the Greene Memorial House was no longer needed as a rectory but as a private home. During this early period in the twentieth century, the house

St. Barnabas wooden church was destroyed by fire in 1911. Church services were held at the Greene Memorial House until the new church was built. *Dorothy Mayor Collection.*

was heated by steam from the Apponaug Co., which was next to the house. A pipe ran from the factory to the house and carried steam until a gas-fired burner was installed. In 1933, the Red Cross, Warwick Chapter, was allowed to use the building. In 1958, the Red Cross, Central Rhode Island Chapter, purchased the building and remained there for a number of decades.

The house was the property of Russell Howard during the latter part of the twentieth century, and a group of Orthodox Jews used the building as the CHAI Center of Chabad of West Bay. In the early twenty-first century, Ed and Jackie Alger purchased the house and used it as a co-op, where a number of individuals rented bedrooms and shared the common areas of the house, such as the kitchen and dining areas. Apponaug residents are anxious to see what the fate of the building will be when a proposed change in the traffic pattern of the Four Corners goes into effect.

APPONAUG'S "JUDGES ROW"

In addition to the stately home built by Caleb Greene on Centerville Road, there are a number of other fine houses in Apponaug that date back to the same period. A short walk south from the Greene Memorial House and the Four Corners to Apponaug Bridge takes us to what was once a thriving seaport and the area then known as "Judges Row." Many of the buildings have been demolished or moved, with the exception of a fine house at 3351 Post Road and the two handsome Federal-period houses on the east side of Post Road, just beyond the bridge. The restoration of these houses is an indication of the growing concern and pride that has developed in Apponaug in the last two decades of the twentieth century. Great efforts have been made to preserve its rich heritage and to make the village more attractive. The two houses on the south side of the bridge are excellent examples of five-bay, center chimney homes, with fine, pedimented, fanlight doorways, and they have been renovated in the late twentieth century.

THE REMINGTON HOUSE

The house at 3376 Post Road, for many years the property of Landing A, Inc., and later of Paul Lancia and Frank DePetrillo, is currently owned by Michael and Patrick Berek. The handsome old building is now the Remington House, one of Warwick's finest restaurants. The house was once owned by Henry Remington, a Revolutionary War soldier and the son of Thomas

The Remington House restoration and its use as a restaurant is a good example of Apponaug's revitalization. *Warwick Historical Society Collection.*

Remington, a well-known sea captain. Henry, a judge of the Rhode Island Supreme Court from 1801 to 1808 and one of Apponaug's most influential residents, built this house in 1801. In 1828, when Judge Remington, age sixty-five, married his second wife, Lucy Ann Arnold, thirty-nine years his junior, he gave Apponaug one of its most celebrated December-May marriages. Much to the surprise of many of the village gossips, the marriage thrived, and Lucy and the judge spent many happy years together.

The two-and-a-half-story, gable-roofed dwelling was remodeled during the Victorian era, with a large bow window on the south side. Until 1997, the fine old structure had been uninhabited and was used as a storehouse for the building at the rear. This long, low rear building was once the notorious Biff's Café, a favorite haunt of Warwick's quahoggers and rough-and-tumble seamen. During the first half of the twentieth century, the café was noted as Apponaug's "trouble spot," and Saturday night almost always saw the Warwick police force called to the tavern to quell fights and arguments. At one time, police chief Forrest Sprague noted that all communities have the equivalent of Biff's Café, "but in Warwick we are fortunate as it is close to the police station."

Eventually, Biff's Café became the Boathouse Tavern and, along with the main house, part of the Remington House restaurant. The restaurant specializes in American and Italian food. Many of the finest features of the old house have been preserved, and now the Remington House has been renovated and transformed into a beautiful Apponaug showplace.

The preservation of the past and the practicality of the present have been admirably brought together.

THE WARNER-HARRISON HOUSE

Next to the Remington House is the lovely, restored, center chimney structure at 3384 Post Road, which is now an office building. This impressive house once belonged to Thomas Warner, a descendant of John Warner, Warwick's first town clerk. John Warner holds the dubious distinction of being the first Warwick resident to be barred from public office and disenfranchised. In 1652, John Warner threatened to kill all the mares in the town, asked Massachusetts to assume control and said that he would "beat out the brains" of a town officer. His descendant, Thomas Warner, 150 years and five generations later, was also town clerk but much more sedate and respected.

It is believed that the house was built in the late eighteenth century and that Thomas Warner added the Federal-period doorway. Warner left the house to his daughter, Catherine, who married sea captain William Harrison. The Warner-Harrison House has been restored by the Architectural Preservation Group. Research by Steve Tyson, whose firm has done the restoration, indicates that the Warner-Harrison House was not only a fine dwelling during much of the nineteenth century, but was also probably, at one time, a funeral parlor. Tyson has found paint scrapings that indicate that one of the large rooms was painted red and black, which would be in keeping with the concept of a nineteenth-century funeral parlor. In addition, the north wall once had a large opening that could have been used to bring in large objects such as caskets. There is also evidence that points to woodworking apparatus that would not be incongruous with the idea of casket making. Fine houses such as this one are excellent examples of how practical and adaptable our early buildings have been. The Harrison family, after ownership of over a century, sold the house in 1920. During much of the late twentieth century, it was owned by Landing A, Inc.

THE ARNOLD HOUSE

One of Apponaug's early landmarks, the Arnold House met a different fate, as the area south of Apponaug Four Corners has witnessed a great deal of change during the last two decades of the twentieth century. A new Walgreens now occupies the area where the S&S Drugstore and I.M. Gan's grocery and package store once stood. One of the village's finest houses, the Arnold residence, in danger of being demolished, has been dismantled and moved to nearby Buttonwoods. The original owner of this house, Thomas Arnold, was one of Apponaug's early residents and a descendant of the Arnolds who were so prominent in Warwick's early history.

Steve Tyson's Architectural Preservation Group has been able to save the Arnold House, which was once located across from the Remington and Warner-Harrison Houses on Post Road. It was at one time one of the most imposing residences south of the Four Corners. At one point, an itinerant artist visited the house and, perhaps in exchange for room and board, painted a mural for its owners that has been discovered and restored by Steve Tyson. The house itself has been moved to Mill Wheel Road in Buttonwoods and has been beautifully restored.

In addition to work done on the Warner-Harrison and Remington Houses on the southeastern side of Post Road, another major restoration has taken place on what was once known as "Judges Row." The two-and-a-half-story, gable-roofed structure on the north side of the bridge at 3351 Post Road has been restored by architect Robert Stirling Morris. Most villagers are very pleased to see this old building take on a new aspect, and they appreciate its owner's concern for preserving one of the area's oldest structures. From the 1940s until 1986, it was known as the Central Café and was more indicative of the changes that befell Apponaug in the mid-twentieth century than representative of its earlier heritage. Mr. Morris, in his restoration, has uncovered some very interesting facts about the building. He believes that it was once a tidal mill, perhaps for snuff manufacturing, before it became a residence about 1743. The old chestnut beams, the mortise and tenon–type construction, the unbroken foundation under the original section and other signs indicate that the structure is over 250 years old and may be one of the oldest buildings in Apponaug.

The Town Workhouse

As might be expected, not everyone was prosperous, and Warwick had its share of the indigent and the helpless. One visual reminder of that aspect can be seen on Colonial Avenue, not far from Post Road. This is the old town workhouse, built in 1765. Colonial Rhode Island followed the example set in England for the care of the poor. Old Elizabethan laws placed the responsibility on local governments and called for towns and parishes to build workhouses to care for the "lame…olde, blynde [and] poor." This modest gable-roofed structure, set gable-end to the street, was Warwick's answer to its growing number of indigent citizens. Despite age and other infirmities, the hapless inhabitants of the poorhouse were made to work at whatever tasks they were capable of performing. By today's standards, the conditions in the workhouse would be considered extremely demeaning and harsh. By 1841, the small house could no longer handle the increasing number of poor and unfortunates, and a new, larger poorhouse and farm was established in Buttonwoods. The house became a private dwelling, and after 1875, it was divided into two tenements that were rented to millworkers.

IMMIGRATION

When the once lucrative sea trade declined in Apponaug in the nineteenth century, the village began to take on a new dimension due to the rise of the textile industry and the coming of the Stonington Railroad. In June 1835, the first train in Rhode Island ran between Boston and Providence. Within two and a half years, the Stonington Railroad, extending south through the state, was open for travel. In 1848, the name was changed from the Stonington Railroad to the New York, Providence and Boston line. In 1893, this railroad merged with the New York, New Haven and Hartford system.

In addition to bringing many advantages to Apponaug's textile industry, the railroad brought in a tide of immigration, which was to alter the old fabric of the village and bring in unimaginable changes. In the 1830s, demand for labor to build the roads witnessed large numbers of Irish Catholics immigrating to Rhode Island. Old prejudices surfaced, and a period of culture shock engulfed Apponaug. The Irish were encamped at Sweet-Meadow Brook, adjacent to the railroad tracks in Apponaug. When the railroad was completed, some of the Irish remained in Warwick to work in the mills. Many of them went to the western section and, by the late nineteenth century, became a dominant force in areas such as Crompton, Centerville, Clyde and Phenix. Later in the century, the railroads carried large numbers of French-Canadians to the Pawtuxet Valley and many emigrants from Sweden and Italy to the Pontiac Mill.

APPONAUG: THE MUNICIPAL CENTER

While the mills were of the utmost importance in creating the village of Apponaug, the growing significance of the area as Warwick's municipal center in the nineteenth century had an impact as well. From the very early colonial period, the desire for a town house was evident. Early records indicate that private homes were used for the first meetings, and by the end of the eighteenth century, the town had grown to the point where town meetings were held at various taverns or inns, as taverns were among the few establishments that contained rooms large enough for public meetings.

The initial phase in the development of the town began when the administrative center of Warwick moved westward from the coast at Old Warwick. This move came about during the Revolutionary War, when the British stopped the ferry that ran from Warwick Neck to Providence and Newport, thereby interrupting the old mail and primary trade routes. With this main artery blocked, the Old Pequot Path (Post Road), which ran through Apponaug, became the most important route. Apponaug, which had been of some significance as a colonial port and as the site of a fulling mill and gristmill, became the focus of Warwick's trade and industry in the nineteenth century.

As the town population grew from 2,532 in 1800 to 5,529 in 1830, the western section, which included the area that is now West Warwick, witnessed the greatest growth. In 1834, Apponaug, as both the economic and geographic center, was the natural selection for the permanent town house and town clerk's office. The old buildings, built in 1834–35, were on the site now occupied by City Hall. They included the town house, clerk's office and outbuildings used to shelter horses and wagons. After the Civil War, Warwick's prosperity continued, and it became obvious that the old town house, clerk's office and outbuildings could no longer be repaired and had to be replaced.

In 1892, the town council met at the office of Enos Lapham, owner of the Centerville Mill. Lapham, then a power in both the textile industry and the political scene, was able to persuade the five-man council to go ahead with plans for a new building.

The result of the council's action was the new Town Hall (present City Hall). This mansard-roofed building, with its ornate façade and five tall chimneys, has been Warwick's pride for many years. The 1893 structure is an excellent example of the Colonial Revival style of the late Victorian era.

Warwick's rapid growth during the first half of the twentieth century took a great toll on the interior of the building. Fortunately, when former mayor Joseph Walsh asked every community action group for priorities on the revitalization of Warwick, all voted for the restoration of City Hall as the focal point. Thanks to the renovation and improvements that began in the 1980s, Apponaug can boast one of the finest city halls in Rhode Island.

The Compston family's long connection with Apponaug dates to the nineteenth century. Here family members stand before the 1834 Town Hall. *Dorothy Mayor Collection.*

Separation of 1913

By the turn of the century, it was obvious that the mill villages in the western section of Warwick and the agricultural eastern section no longer had the same interests, and a separation was called for on both economic and political grounds. In spite of many shrewd political moves to halt the split, Warwick's third, fourth and fifth representative districts were chartered as the town of West Warwick in 1913. The division created a number of questions regarding schools and buildings. Part of the agreement between the two towns resulted in the Warwick High School on Providence Street, built in 1905, going to the new town, while Warwick kept control of the 1893 Town Hall.

The Oriental Print Works Comes to Apponaug

No history of Apponaug can be told without relating the village to the mills that grew and thrived there. As noted earlier, the textile manufacturing business that Caleb Greene established in Apponaug in 1809 prospered for a time. By the second half of the nineteenth century, however, the Greene mills had suffered some financial reverses, and the owners were persuaded to sell out their interests. This enabled a new group of entrepreneurs, led by Alfred Augustus Reed, to move into the area.

Alfred A. Reed made his fortune in the East India trade. After 1857, Reed, whose business took him to the Far East, established the Oriental Mills north of Providence. In seeking a better location for the enterprise, one of his partners, Edward D. Boit, found Apponaug a most desirable site for the establishment of a print works. Boit told Reed that Apponaug was an ideal place, as "the situation is healthy and pretty good for help and cheap for living and as fine a location as any other for Steam Cotton Mills."

The establishment of such a large enterprise as the Oriental Print Works meant a number of changes in Apponaug. In addition to the Greene textile mill, the purchase by Reed and his partners included one large tenement house, two smaller ones, hotels and boardinghouses. The mill attracted large numbers of workers, including many Irish and French Catholics. The increased activity saw Apponaug once again revitalized and an important center for business and trade.

By the early twentieth century, motor vehicles were adding to the traffic problem at the Four Corners. Officer Al Izzi, "the human windmill," is directing the flow of traffic. *Dorothy Mayor Collection.*

THE PANIC OF 1873

The prosperity from the Oriental Print Works declined in 1873. This was the year of a very serious panic, or depression, which had a devastating effect on Rhode Island. The collapse of the A. & W. Sprague Manufacturing Co. in that year seriously curtailed the textile industry for a time. The man behind the success of the print works in Apponaug, Alfred A. Reed, died in 1879. By 1883, the company had ceased to operate and many of the mill hands were once again unemployed.

THE APPONAUG PRINT WORKS

Fortunately, the period in which the mill was closed was of short duration. The company was able to continue in operation after 1896. At that time, it was known as the Apponaug Print Works. This company enjoyed a limited success until 1913, when, under the leadership of J.P. Farnsworth, it made a major change and began a period of unprecedented prosperity. Farnsworth and his colleagues decided to direct the company toward the development of finishing processes for fine textiles instead of staple fabrics. This field, which eventually included the finer grades of cotton, rayon, Celanese and mixed fabrics, required a greater technical skill and more delicate workmanship. Fortunately, the company was able to acquire the skills of Alfred L. Lustig, one of the world's foremost color chemists.

Lustig Comes to the Apponaug Mill

Lustig is generally given credit for making the Apponaug Company one of the leading firms in the textile industry. His brilliance and innovations proved to be more than adequate to meet the challenges of the early twentieth century. In 1917, when J.P. Farnsworth died, Lustig was made president of the company. Under his leadership, the Apponaug plant became a major employer in Warwick, attracting skilled workers from nearby Natick, Clyde and Riverpoint.

It was during the early years of Lustig's management that the mills witnessed a great deal of prosperity because of World War I. The war that started in Europe in 1914 caused an unprecedented demand for American goods, and when the United States entered the conflict in 1917, many young men from

The early Oriental Print Works was taken over by the Apponaug Company, which expanded the mills in the twentieth century. *Warwick Historical Society Collection.*

World War I meant a great deal to Apponaug. The "doughboy" statue on the City Hall lawn reminds us of that fact.

the mill villages along the Pawtuxet River entered the army, thereby causing a labor shortage. This tight labor market gave greater bargaining power to the workers, and they eventually forced the textile companies to abandon the sixty-four-hour week for a forty-eight-hour one with higher wages.

While other mills in the Pawtuxet Valley were often unable to compete with England and Europe, the mill in Apponaug was successful. Much of this was because the print works, engaged in bleaching and dyeing, depended a great deal on the water supply and the skill of the chemists. Both were needed, and as stated so well by the owners of the Oriental Print Works, the water from Gorton's Pond was excellent. Another reason for success was the fact that the location of the large complex was within easy reach of the principal textile mills and the most important wholesale markets. This was significant, as during the first part of the twentieth century the Apponaug Company's business was done entirely for mills and converters.

To keep pace with major changes and innovations, the Apponaug Company plant underwent a major modernization between 1920 and 1928. This surprised a number of mill owners, as it was a time when other mills were talking of closing. Because of this, the Apponaug Company, unlike other mills during the trying years of the Great Depression, found itself the recipient of increased orders during the 1930s

The importance of the Lustigs to Rhode Island's economy often prompted full cooperation from the State of Rhode Island. One example of this came during a Lustig family emergency in 1931. At that time, Alfred L. Lustig, who was vacationing in Virginia, was stricken with stomach ulcers and had to undergo surgery. Republican governor Norman S. Case offered the assistance of the state. As a result, Mrs. Lustig and her daughter, Mrs. Frederick C. Brown of Apponaug, were escorted by state police on an exceedingly fast trip to New York City so that they could catch the earliest train south. Thanks to this cooperation, Mrs. Lustig was able to get to her husband's bedside before the emergency operation.

The End of an Era

In 1935, Alfred L. Lustig, the president and general manager of the Apponaug Company, died. The Lustig family continued to control the enterprise until 1944, when it sold the mill to George V. Mechan. The Apponaug Company eventually became a victim of the decline in the textile industry that had started in the 1920s. In January 1958, Frederick G. Brown announced that the company would close its doors on March 15. More than two years went by before the vast complex, with its ten buildings, water tower and power plants, was sold. In 1960, the Anchor Realty Co. purchased the property and

The difficult times of the Great Depression brought WPA workers to Apponaug's Four Corners for much-needed repairs. *Warwick Historical Society Collection.*

soon began renting the space to diverse industries. Far from being obsolete, the Apponaug mills had demonstrated that there was a demand for the buildings despite the near death of the textile industry.

The Terrible Fires

In mid-February 1961, however, the first of three spectacular fires occurred, and the remaining days of the Apponaug mill complex were numbered. The fire, which most likely started in the dye house, quickly destroyed one building and badly damaged two others. Firefighters feared that the spectacular tongues of flame, which illuminated the night sky and could be seen two miles away, would consume the entire complex and part of the village of Apponaug as well. The efforts to put out the fire were hampered by the difficulty of access between the buildings and by the piles of snow on the ground. This 1961 fire was the worst in Warwick's history to that time.

Five years later, in November 1966, another fire at the Apponaug complex occurred. This time it came when the 175-foot water tower was struck by lightning and burst into flames. The blaze burned for several hours before it was finally extinguished. Fortunately, firemen were able to put up a water screen, and when the weather improved, a state helicopter was used to smother the fire with a water-and-detergent mixture.

In September 1969, fire again struck in Apponaug at a time when there were thirty-three small businesses in the complex. This time, the buildings were almost totally destroyed. The main difficulty in controlling this fire was the inadequate water supply. The fire chief at the time, Thomas E. Duckworth, explained why the 1969 fire was so much more devastating than the one in 1961. He said that the water in the mill trench in 1961 was high and supplied the firemen with thousands of gallons of water, while in September 1969 it was nearly dry. He went on to say, "I had the equipment, but what could I do? When I put more lines on, I just robbed from one to give to another."

Twenty-first-Century Optimism

The future of the Apponaug mill complex site is now in the hands of the Sawtooth Associates LLC. In an interview with the *Warwick Beacon* in August 2004, Brandon Bell, president of the company, said, "It's a work in progress. A lot of people passing by would call it an eyesore as it is now." He added, "There is potential here, you just need to find it." All of Apponaug is waiting.

Apponaug

Apponaug at the City's Center

The two decades after the 1913 separation of Warwick into two towns saw an increased growth in Warwick to the degree that the town meeting form of government had become too unwieldy. The result was a move to adopt a city form of government. It was only after a great number of heated debates, and two unsuccessful attempts, that Warwick was able to get a municipal charter in 1931. In January 1933, the Town Hall officially became the City Hall. Pierce H. Brereton became the first mayor, and the city councilmen took office.

As the new city witnessed the problems of the Great Depression, the Hurricane of 1938 and World War II, many of the fine old buildings in Apponaug suffered from overcrowding and neglect. It was feared that many of the old buildings in the town would completely disappear as a result of the demand for housing and industry. Fortunately, Warwick has had a number of citizens who have been very concerned with the preservation of historic homes and buildings. In the 1970s, concerned citizens, led by David Stackhouse, were successful in starting the Warwick Preservation Commission.

In addition to the City Hall at 3275 Post Road, the former Kentish Artillery Armory (3259 Post Road) and the Henry Warner Budlong

Recently, a kayaker propelled her craft in Apponaug Cove, much like the Indians would have done in the seventeenth century.

Memorial Library (3267 Post Road) compose the Warwick Civic Center historic district. Apponaug also has three historically important churches along Post Road. These churches—the Warwick Central Baptist Church (1834), St. Barnabas Episcopal Church (1921–26) and St. Catherine's Roman Catholic Church (1916)—add variety to the area and supply the diverse needs of the community.

The city of Warwick is fortunate in having a number of historic buildings in a relatively small area in Apponaug. This makes it possible for visitors to take a walking tour of the historic Apponaug Village and enjoy the varied architecture that has spanned two centuries.

CONIMICUT

Thus, before two years had elapsed, the purchasers of Warwick, with the exception of Sampson Shoten, who had died, found themselves in a Boston prison and their families dispersed, they knew not where.
—*Oliver Payson Fuller,* History of Warwick, *1875*

Conimicut, a thriving and picturesque area along Warwick's shore, is one of the villages that can trace its history back to the founding of Warwick in 1643. The story begins with Samuel Gorton and his followers and their quest to find a safe haven where they could practice their beliefs without persecution.

Upon arriving in Massachusetts in 1637, Samuel Gorton, Warwick's charismatic founder, quickly antagonized an impressive list of influential and powerful persons. This fascinating and enigmatic character was brilliant but unorthodox. As a self-proclaimed preacher, he severely criticized the religious doctrines of the Boston and Plymouth Puritans and opposed their right to rule in Massachusetts. For a time, his brilliance and appeal were tolerated, but as he challenged all authority, he was banished from Massachusetts and eventually made his way to Providence. His views on government and legal rights soon led him to quarrel with a number of leaders in the community. Among the enemies he made were William Arnold, William Harris and other early settlers of Pawtuxet Village.

Mainly because of Arnold, Gorton's attempt to be admitted as a freeman in Providence failed. Arnold, on May 25, 1641, wrote that Gorton "showed himself an insolent, railing and turbulent person." Even Roger Williams, usually a tolerant man, found Gorton troublesome. Roger Williams, in a

The pride of the residents of Conimicut is reflected in these attractive signs welcoming all to the historic village.

letter to Governor Winthrop dated "Providence 1640," wrote, "Master Gorton having abused high and low at Aquidnick, is now bewitching and bemadding poor Providence."

When Gorton and his followers attempted to move into the Pawtuxet area, three of the original Pawtuxet purchasers offered themselves and their land to the protection of Massachusetts in September 1642 to keep Gorton from settling in the colony. The Gortonists then moved to the land south of Pawtuxet called Shawomet to be beyond the limits of Providence and Pawtuxet. Here, in November 1642, they purchased the Shawomet lands now known as Warwick, West Warwick and Coventry from the Native Americans.

THE SHAWOMET PURCHASE

On January 12, 1642–43, Gorton and eleven of his followers signed a deed known as the Shawomet Purchase with Miantonomi, the "chief sachem of the Narragansetts." The purchase included about ninety square miles of territory, or approximately sixty thousand acres. In the spring of 1643, thanks to the purchase and good will of the Narragansett leaders, Gorton and his followers settled at Mill Creek, which borders the area just south of Conimicut Point. The Gortonites sent for their wives and children and began to build a small community along the Conimicut shore. According to the principles of their leader, the settlers agreed to live together "in voluntary association" rather than establish a formal government. Their happiness in forming a settlement to their liking, unfortunately, was short-lived, as their small village was attacked and nearly annihilated.

The Massachusetts Involvement

The "Pawtuxet Men," led by William Arnold, hoping to drive Gorton from Shawomet, convinced Pomham, sachem of Shawomet, and Socononoco, sachem of Pawtuxet, to place their lands under Massachusetts jurisdiction. To do so, they had to deny that they had assented to Miantonomi's sale of the lands to the Gortonists. Massachusetts claimed that an act of submission to its government by any party extended its jurisdiction over that party's lands. This gave Massachusetts the opportunity to increase its influence in Narragansett Bay. The Massachusetts General Court sent a letter to the purchasers of Shawomet demanding their presence before the court. The Gortonists refused, and Massachusetts took action by sending Captain Cook with forty soldiers to Warwick.

Shawomet Under Attack

As soon as they felt that their families were safe, the Gortonists fortified one of the houses south of Conimicut Point and prepared to defend it. On October 3, 1643, the cattle of the Shawomet men were seized and the assault began. After several days, the Gortonists felt that they had no choice but to surrender to the superior force. The action that followed has been described as one of the most disgraceful episodes in English colonial history. Gorton and his followers were roughly handled, carried off as prisoners to Boston and tried on charges of "heresy and sedition." Gorton, along with six of his followers, was put in irons and sent to work in various towns. After a very humiliating and brutal winter, Gorton and his men were set free but banished from all territory under the jurisdiction of Massachusetts and Plymouth colonies.

The court claimed that this included Providence and Shawomet. It ruled that Gorton had to leave Shawomet or he would be put to death.

The Gortonists were fortunate in finding refuge on Aquidneck Island, which was beyond Massachusetts jurisdiction. The result of the unjust seizure of the Gortonists not only changed the attitude of the colonists on Aquidneck Island, but it also had an effect on the Narragansett Indians. They were amazed that Gorton was set free and believed that the "Gortonoges," as they called them, had more powerful friends in England than did the English of Massachusetts.

Believing that Gorton, a friend of their slain leader Miantonomi, had great influence in the English court, the Narragansett tribe, upon Gorton's suggestion, placed itself under "the government and protection of that honorable State of Old England" and made Gorton and his followers their agents to report their submission to the king.

ROBERT RICH, EARL OF WARWICK

During the winter of 1644–45, Gorton, accompanied by Randall Holden and John Greene, set sail for England and presented his case before Parliament. There, thanks to the influence of Robert Rich, Earl of Warwick and governor in chief of Foreign Plantations, the lands were restored to the Gortonites. In honor of the earl, the Gortonites changed the name of the colony from Shawomet to Warwick.

THE TENEMENT AT CONIMICUT

The settlers found that while the danger of a Massachusetts takeover was no longer a threat, life in the small town was fraught with difficulties. Among these were problems from both humans and animals. Because of difficulties with some of the Shawomet Indian tribe and wolves, Conimicut Point was selected as an area to keep the settlers' animals at night. Harold R. Curtis, in his historical sketch *Tenement on Conimicut*, tells us that

> *by constructing a fence across the head of the neck from the Mill Cove directly north to the shore of Narragansett Bay, a distance of not more than nine hundred feet, an excellent pasture of almost two hundred acres would be provided...Here the cattle of the Gortonists could graze in comparative security and with little danger of escaping into the wild country inland.*

The waters at Conimicut Point contain dangerous shoals that kept enemies away from the cattle. It wasn't until 1858 that a beacon was erected there. This lighthouse was built in 1882. *Warwick Historical Society Collection.*

The word tenement then had a different meaning than it does today. "Tenement" meant a house and land share, and it was granted to Thomas Thornicraft. According to the first book of Warwick records, he received eight acres of land at Conimicut upon the condition that he maintain a fence, which was often called a "water fence."

Mill Cove

As many of the early settlers in Conimicut and Warwick Neck were farmers, it soon became obvious that there was a need for a gristmill to grind the corn and wheat. Using the power of the tides at Mill Cove, Thomas Safford and a number of other early proprietors were given permission to build a gristmill and to grind corn for the inhabitants. Their fee was to be two quarts of grain per bushel, and this became Warwick's first industrial enterprise. It was also the cause of the first complaint. Charges were made by some of the settlers that the mill owners were using too large a measure for their fee. In the 1650s, the records show "it being complained of that the Toll Dish is to [*sic*] big."

Stone Enders

Settlers in and around Conimicut Point saw some prosperity in the early years. They erected houses, called "stone enders," and through hard work began to see their farms prosper. These stone enders made use of timber and stone, both of which were in abundance in the area. The houses were usually timber framed and one and a half or two stories in height, with one room on each floor. One end of the house contained a massive stone chimney, which usually filled the entire end wall, thus giving the dwelling its name. The windows were very small and filled with oiled paper, and the stairs to the upper chambers were steep and usually squeezed in between the chimney and the front entrance.

King Philip's War

This brief period of prosperity was disrupted in 1675, when the united colonies of Massachusetts Bay, Plymouth and Connecticut invaded Rhode Island during King Philip's War. Rhode Island was not included among the united colonies, but for the period of early hostilities, the colonists in Warwick felt safe due to the friendly relations between Samuel Gorton and the Narragansetts. However, after the Great Swamp massacre in South Kingstown, the Narragansetts joined the Wampanoags, and in March 1676, Warwick was attacked. The settlers fled to the safety of Portsmouth, and all of the houses in the town, with the exception of Thomas Greene's Stone Castle, were burned. By October 1676, all of the major Indian leaders had been killed or captured and the war was over. In the spring of 1677, the people of Conimicut returned to their homes (or what was left of them).

With an increase in population and an end to the Indian problem, it became obvious that if the town was to grow and supply the needs of its people, the water power and other resources to the west would have to be developed. The old sawmill at Mill Cove had been destroyed by the Indians; the grinding stones had been smashed, as many of the Indians believed that this was a symbol of the power of the English. Once the war was over, however, it was obvious to the returning settlers that the mills at Mill Cove and Tuskatucket Brook (at the head of Brush Neck Cove) were not adequate to meet the demands of the inhabitants. Early in 1677–78, a grant was made to establish a sawmill along the Pawtuxet River. Many members of the younger generation moved from Conimicut toward Apponaug and the west, as there was more land available and greater opportunities.

While this was happening, much of the land in Conimicut was being settled by the descendants of the Greene and Arnold families. John Greene, surgeon, and Stephen Arnold had large parcels of land, and they willed much of their property to their children. By this time, there was no longer a need for the "tenement at Conimicut" or the water fence. Animals were now free to graze along the Four-Mile Common between Conimicut and Apponaug. As a result, the land of the old "tenement," which abutted that of the Greene family, was purchased by Stephen Arnold in 1680. In that same year, Arnold's daughter Elizabeth (1659–1728) married Peter Greene (1654–1723).

After King Philip's War ended, Peter Greene returned to Conimicut and took an active part in Warwick politics. As there was still fear of attack by enemies, he became very active in the "Train Band" of local militia and, in 1697, became captain of the unit. In 1699, Stephen Arnold died, and two of his Conimicut lots, including the tenement lands, went to his daughter Elizabeth. That property passed into the Greene family. Historians of the area believe that Peter Greene may have built a house on the tenement lands as early as 1714. In 1750, that house was replaced by the home that now stands at 1124 West Shore Road at the corner of Economy Avenue. The house is an excellent visual reminder of a basic colonial "five-room plan" with a huge center chimney, and for many generations it was the center of a prosperous farm.

In 1800, the farmhouse passed to Judge Steven Greene, who left the house to his daughter, Marcy, who married Captain James Warner. The old homestead remained in the Greene-Warner family for two more generations. In 1864, it was sold to Cyrus Harris of the Greene Manufacturing Company, ending nine generations and two hundred years of ownership by the "Greenes of Conimicut." Eventually, the farm passed to Maria M. (Harris) Foster in 1883. It has since been owned by a number of other families, including Michael and Arlene Hebert, who were responsible for much of the work of renovating the building in the 1980s.

Smuggling Activities

Another of the interesting houses in Conimicut Village is the Moses Greene House at 11 Economy Avenue. This house was connected to the triangular trade, smuggling and the slave trade during the period in which the house was owned by members of the Lippitt and Greene families. Like the Captain Peter Greene House at 1124 West Shore Road, this house was built about

1750. The two houses are so similar that it is believed they were the work of the same builder. The histories of the two houses differ, however, as the Moses Greene House is rich in the seafaring lore of Warwick. While the primary interest in the colony during the eighteenth century remained agriculture, Warwick's proximity to the bay caused a number of its leading families to turn to the sea for their livelihoods.

During this period, Warwick increased its agricultural products by the western settlements. Much of the produce from these farms, as well as those from Conimicut, were shipped to Newport and Providence from ports along Warwick's shore, and the colony became a significant part of the ever-growing sea trade.

Much of the prosperity that came to the colony was due to the leadership of Major John Greene Jr. Major John Greene was annually elected deputy governor from 1690 to 1700. Major Greene is regarded as a champion for Rhode Island rights and especially as the man who introduced Rhode Island to the controversial practice of using privateers. As England was at war for over thirty years in the 1690–1763 period, there was a demand that merchant ships arm themselves to make war on the mother country's enemies. As an incentive, ships receiving privateer commissions were allowed to keep a large portion of the spoils of war. A number of Greene family men in Conimicut did take to the sea and engaged in the wars of the mother colony. Privateering, as one can imagine, brought high profits but was a very precarious profession.

The Triangular Trade

The role played by privateers, with all the excitement, was only one of the segments of the lucrative maritime enterprises that were to aid in Warwick's growth as a seaport town. The key to the maritime prosperity was the trade with the West Indies. Through shrewd dealings, enough profit was made by selling cheese, fish, lumber, horses and livestock in order to gather a large enough cargo to trade with the southern colonies and with the West Indies for sugar and molasses. These were distilled into rum, a commodity accepted nearly everywhere. In addition to a large number of distilleries in Newport and Providence, there were also a number of small distilleries all along Warwick's shore. In 1712–13, many of the restrictions placed on the American colonies in regard to the slave trade were removed, and the colonies were now encouraged to participate in this lucrative trade.

Conimicut

Smuggling

In 1733, when the British passed the Molasses Act in an attempt to gain a share in the profits being made by the colonists, Rhode Islanders resorted to smuggling. Mill Cove in Conimicut was well suited for this activity, as small schooners could enter the cove and the illegal goods could be taken to the house at the cove to be stored and distributed. The belief is that Rhode Island ships, after eluding British patrol ships around Beavertail Point in Jamestown, came into Mill Cove to unload their contraband goods. From there, in smaller boats and under cover of darkness, the goods could be sent to Providence or Newport. Later, when there were attempts to curtail the slave trade, Warwick, Newport and Providence resorted to the smuggling of humans as well. The discovery of chains in the cellar of the Moses Greene House has led to the belief that slaves were kept there at different periods.

England's preoccupation with European wars had a positive effect on Warwick's prosperity, as it was impossible for the mother country to strictly administer the restrictive trade laws or to closely supervise the granting of privileges to privateers. Nearly all of Warwick's inhabitants benefited from the smuggling and increased trade. Those directly concerned with ships and supplies were obvious beneficiaries. In addition, farmers received higher prices, and artisans found a market for their talents as Warwick began supplying the major ports of Newport and Providence. Goods were shipped via a ferry that ran between Warwick Neck and the northern end of Prudence Island and from there to Newport. By 1742, Warwick Neck was a vital link in the postal and commercial trade—a ferry from Providence stopped there and then sailed on to the islands.

After the French and Indian War ended in 1763, England felt that it had the resources to stop the smuggling, and the pressure against the colonists was increased. The trade in rum was so lucrative that Warwick ship captains and owners found that it was more profitable to smuggle than to comply with the law. The many coves and inlets in Warwick, especially those around Warwick Cove, Mill Pond Cove and Pawtuxet, continued to be used for smuggling despite the increased risk. As the British increased their patrols, the gap between the mother country and the colonies grew greater and eventually resulted in a struggle for independence. Rhode Islanders from Conimicut took part in this fight for freedom.

In the decade following the Revolutionary War, there was growing sentiment against the slave trade. In 1787, it became illegal for Rhode Islanders to engage in this "nefarious" trade. Once again, there was smuggling in Mill Cove, and the Moses Greene House may have played a role in this trade. It

The seawall at Conimicut, with its waterfront homes, attracted many affluent professionals and businesspeople to spend summers here at the bay. *Warwick Historical Society Collection.*

Conimicut

should be noted, however, that while smuggling was at times very profitable, it was not the main occupation of the people who lived in the house. Moses Greene, whose name is most closely associated with the house, was primarily engaged in agriculture and was actually born in 1815, after the "glory days" of smuggling had ended.

In the late 1980s, the charming ten-room house was restored as close to its 1750 style as possible by Mrs. Cindy Laboissonniere. The Moses Greene House, spanning a period of over 250 years of Warwick's history, is one of the city's excellent visual reminders of Warwick's heritage.

Conimicut Changes

After the initial growth of Conimicut in the late seventeenth century, the village showed little change from its agricultural and sea trading base until the mid-nineteenth century. When the British stopped the ferry from Warwick Neck to the islands in 1775, these farms suffered. The ferry was an important trade and mail route that connected Warwick to the key ports along the eastern seaboard. As a result of the blockade, Conimicut and other eastern towns declined in importance, and Apponaug, located on the Post Road, became the new center of trade and politics. Conimicut remained primarily farmland, owned in large part by the descendants of the early settlers. This condition existed well into the nineteenth century.

By the late nineteenth century, the western section of the town, now known as West Warwick, developed a thriving textile industry. As this new enterprise prospered, immigrants came to work in the mills, and the center of population moved farther away from Conimicut. The prosperity of the mills and the increasing population brought about a new meaning and use for the lands along Warwick's shore. The affluent merchants and mill owners began to look for large landed estates with a view of the bay. They found that Conimicut was an excellent source of inexpensive land and purchased large acreage for very little capital. Soon, the old farmhouses were replaced by lovely Victorian mansions, and the area changed in its appearance and function.

Mark Rock

During the mid-nineteenth century, steamboats cruising along the bay were enchanted with Warwick's shoreline, and the desire to establish shore resorts came into vogue. While Rocky Point, established by Captain William Winslow in 1847, was the most well-known and largest shore attraction in the area, resorts were also founded in and around Conimicut. Mark Rock, north of Conimicut Point near the present-day Rock Avenue, was the most notorious for many years. The Mark Rock Hotel, like the Longmeadow Hotel south of Conimicut Point, catered for the most part to transient visitors in the late nineteenth century. Unlike Rocky Point, it never attempted to become a "rich man's resort" or an amusement park but rather developed into a drinking and gambling mecca.

The Mark Rock Hotel was located near a large, flat rock, which archaeologists believed bore indications of Indian, or perhaps Scandinavian, hieroglyphics. Steamboats from Providence stopped at the dock near the hotel and unloaded groups of merrymakers. According to newspaper reports of the time, the patrons of the Conimicut resort were "thoroughly disreputable." The excursion boat from Providence brought its passengers to Mark Rock early on Sunday morning and came back in the evening to gather its patrons after a full day of "carousing." It was common, we are told, for a detachment of Providence police to meet the returning boat to arrest the "brawling, intoxicated revelers as they disembarked at the wharf."

The Warwick Railroad and the Trolley

It was a number of years before residents became adamant about changing Conimicut's reputation from being associated with the excesses of Mark Rock to being a respectable community again. It took some time for the village to recover from this unsavory reputation, and much of this change came about with the coming of the Warwick Railroad and the electric trolley. With easy access to Providence and other areas of the state via the trolley lines, Conimicut was being regarded as the ideal suburban setting and a fashionable summer resort. By the late nineteenth century, the railroad station at the intersection of Beach and Transit Streets, long since demolished, was one of the busiest on the Warwick–Oakland Beach line.

Substantial homes, such as those on Beach Avenue in Conimicut, grew in number during the twentieth century as Providence's affluent merchants, doctors and lawyers found it fashionable to have summer homes along the Warwick shore. So, too, did the number of more modest dwellings grow—thanks to the electrification of the line and the increase in the number of trolley cars, it was possible to work in Providence and live in Conimicut. The change in Conimicut was gradual as the old and the new mingled in the early twentieth century. For much of that period, West Shore Road was still commonly called "Apponaug Road," and the slaughterhouse, located just south of Mark Rock, was known for its old-fashioned "shindigs" in the fall. The late Lewis Taft, well-known local historian, remembers the occasions well. As a boy, he chased the "greased pig" with all of the other kids. The family of the boy who caught the pig would be given the animal after it had been butchered. Rural events such as these gradually gave way to different types of entertainments, and Conimicut gradually settled into what was more in accordance with a suburban lifestyle.

WOODBURY UNION CHURCH

Much of the credit for the change can be traced to the beginnings of the Woodbury Union Church. This church began with a small gathering in the Conimicut School in 1906. The first meeting took place on a very stormy Sunday, September 30, 1906. As weather reports and forecasts were in their infancy at the time, it is possible that Warwick may have caught the tail end of a hurricane or tropical storm. In any event, only six people attended the meeting because of the weather. Despite this poor start, word spread through

Commuters at the railroad station found the village easily accessible to other areas of the state. *Donald Skuce Collection (WHS).*

the community, and on the following Sunday, thirty-three persons, both children and adults, attended, and five classes were formed. By December of that year, the number had grown to an enrollment of fifty-five.

The growth and success of the Sunday school prompted discussions among Conimicut residents in relation to establishing a church in the village. At first, this seemed impossible, as there was no established religion in the area and the residents were divided among Baptist, Episcopalian and a scattering of nearly every other religious persuasion found at the time. Undaunted by the great variety of religious beliefs, residents called for a meeting to discuss the building of a church for all people of all religious persuasion and of all ages.

The meeting was an immediate success. A church corporation was formed and plans were made to erect a suitable building. Mrs. Ida Wright donated the land for the building as a memorial to Mr. Woodbury, her father. The church corporation soon after selected the name Woodbury Union Church of Conimicut. It was so named in honor of Mr. Woodbury and also to indicate that it was interdenominational. The church's cornerstone was laid on November 9, 1907. The development of the church and the village closely parallel each other, as for many years the Woodbury Union Church was the center of community life. As the church congregation grew, it became necessary to have a regular pastor. This was not accomplished until 1925, when the Reverend A. Gordon Batstone, a student at Gordon College in Boston, came to the church. During the next twelve years, the church witnessed a large growth in membership, four pastors, a crippling fire and rebuilding.

In 1938, disaster struck Conimicut in the form of a hurricane and tidal wave. The Woodbury Union Church aided the many victims in the area and allowed the building to be used by the National Guard as a headquarters for ten days during the period following the devastating storm. During World War II, the church was again used by outside agencies, such as the Red Cross, as a canteen.

In February 1948, the Woodbury Union Church, which had been interdenominational since its founding in 1907, became the Woodbury Union Church, Presbyterian. The choice to become united with a major denomination came as a result of the difficulties that the church experienced in getting ministers to leave their chosen denominations to become pastor of a Union church. The church became part of the Congregation of Presbyterian Churches, USA, but it retained the word "Union," as it was still an ecumenical congregation and that point was emphasized.

The church has had many outstanding pastors; one of the most recent came in 1972. He was the Reverend William G. Lover, who preached his

The Woodbury Union Church and its pastors, then and now, have long been an integral part of the growth of Conimicut Village.

first sermon at the church on the first Sunday in December of that year. Richard Deering, in his church history *Our Presbyterian Years*, notes that while the pastor was preaching, the lights went out. Undaunted, the Reverend Lover continued, and when he reached a point in his text that read "Let there be light," the lights came back on. It was later learned that a squirrel had gotten into a transformer and short-circuited the wiring. It certainly made for a dramatic beginning for the new pastor.

To say that the Reverend Lover played a major role in the continued development of the church and the community is a definite understatement. Under his leadership, Conimicut became more acutely aware of the historical aspects of the village. He and Conimicut activist Eileen Naughton were responsible for organizing a group to work toward restoring much of the beauty to the village and many other community-related activities.

As in the past, under the Reverend Lover, and today under Pastor Beth Appel, the church opened its doors to many organizations, including Cub Scouts, Boy Scouts, Girl Scouts and Alcoholics Anonymous, to name a few. The Woodbury Union Church, Presbyterian, today continues to work within the spirit of ecumenism. The church takes part in Thanksgiving services along with a number of other churches and also invites other churches to

During the late nineteenth and early twentieth centuries children played at growing up. This mock wedding by a Sunday school class provided spiritual values as well as entertainment. *Dorothy Andrews Collection (WHS).*

participate in the local food bank, which the Woodbury Union Church founded. Without doubt, and with much enthusiasm, the Woodbury Union Church, Presbyterian, serves as a vital part of the community in Conimicut as it did in 1907, when it was first organized.

Conimicut Volunteer Fire Company

As the volume of passengers on the trolley lines continued to grow and more houses were being built, it became necessary to increase the fire protection in the village. One of the most important and colorful of all the volunteer fire companies in Warwick during the early twentieth century was the one in Conimicut. On January 11, 1911, a meeting of the Conimicut Rural Improvement Society put a plan into action for a fire company. Thirty-six men signed the rolls as volunteers at that time. Arthur W. Coffin was selected as the first foreman, or chief, and a hand-drawn truck was purchased to carry brooms, shovels, fire extinguishers and other pieces of equipment. According to a 1960 report on volunteer fire companies, the Conimicut Volunteer Fire Company had a horse-drawn wagon. The report goes on to say, "In these days it is said that the first man to arrive at the fire barn with a horse to pull the apparatus was paid $1.00 for each fire." When the alarm was sounded, the rush was on, as one dollar represented a tidy sum at the time.

A firehouse was erected on Ocean Avenue (now Ardway Avenue) in 1915. In addition to facing the many problems that beset other volunteer companies, Conimicut's proximity to the bay added the danger of high winds and hurricanes. The company was really put to the test during the Hurricane of 1938. Conimicut was severely damaged by the storm—123 houses were destroyed and twenty-two persons lost their lives. The Conimicut Volunteer Fire Company provided prestigious and continuous service for twenty-three days. In addition to offering fire protection, more than forty-two members of the company assisted in relocating residents to shelter and aided the police in maintaining order. In 1954, when three hurricanes hit the village, the company was able to evacuate all residents, and as a result, there was no loss of life. In 1956, the Conimicut Volunteer Fire Company became part of the Warwick Fire Department, and since that time, the old firehouse has been remodeled into a private home.

Conimicut: A Modern Village

As noted by Conimicut historians, the growth and popularity of the village was due to the electrification of the old Warwick Railroad and the creation of the trolley. One of the many attractions for both year-round residents and many day-trippers was the Conimicut Casino. In 1906, it was a thriving enterprise enjoyed by young and old. The nostalgia surrounding the casino has lived on long after the building was demolished. For many, the memories of bowling and taking part in other activities at this facility recapture the fun of rainy summer days. Conimicut during the early twentieth century was, however, much more than a place for summer pleasure. It was also beginning to develop as a desirable place to work, worship and raise a family.

St. Benedict's Church

As the trolley brought more and more Roman Catholics to the area, the need for a Catholic church became apparent. As a result, St. Benedict's Church was established in 1914. The early St. Benedict's Church was housed in a small building on Beach Avenue, not far from the railroad station and the post office. At first, the congregation was small, patronized mainly by

The post office in the village not only served the obvious function, but it was also a place where neighbors met and chatted while getting their mail. *Warwick Historical Society Collection.*

summer visitors. The ability to live in Conimicut and to work in Providence or elsewhere soon brought working families to the area to enjoy the suburban community. Irish, Italian and French immigrants, once confined to living in the mill villages, now found Conimicut more to their liking, and the number of Catholics attending St. Benedict's Church increased rapidly, creating a need for expansion. A new church was built in 1973. In the manner of the Woodbury Union Church, St. Benedict's became a vital part of community life and the center of activity for many. It is especially noted for the excellent work it does with a special religious education program for mentally challenged people of all ages.

Conimicut Grammar School

Along with the influx of new residents came the necessity for schools. Conimicut's wood-framed schoolhouse at 820 West Shore Road was Colonial Revival in style to keep in accordance with the village's heritage. The new residents of the village were very pleased to find a well-built, functioning schoolhouse in the center of the village, but soon that, too, was inadequate at meeting their needs. In 1925, Gothic-style wings were added to the Conimicut School. During the 1920s, it seemed that all children in Conimicut and the surrounding area went to the same school, had the same teachers, read the same books, engaged in the same activities and enjoyed a common culture that carried them through the difficult times of the Great Depression and World War II.

After World War II, the old wooden building in Conimicut gave way to the more modern schools and was no longer used for educating youngsters. The building continued to function well into the late twentieth century, however, in another significant capacity. For many years, the building served as a health center, dedicated to Dr. John Ferris, a much-beloved Warwick physician. For many years, the building at 821 West Shore Road was part of the Elizabeth Buffum Chace Center, which provided outreach services and education for community residents and victims of domestic violence. The center was named in honor of Elizabeth Buffum Chace, a nineteenth-century crusader for human rights and the abolition of slavery.

Recently, the City of Warwick has donated the old Conimicut School buildings to be utilized as a new center that will provide elder services, support groups, court advocacy and individual and group counseling. At the opening of the center, Mayor Scott Avedisian commented that "these issues and societal problems will not be swept under the rug in our city. Our people look to one another with care and concern." These words mirror the feelings that the Conimicut School has inspired for many decades.

CONIMICUT POINT PARK AND LIGHTHOUSE

The point at Conimicut, which is now the site of one of Warwick's loveliest parks, has always been an important part of the village's history. It was first called Shawomet, and near here was the first settlement. For much of the early colonial period, the settlers kept their animals here to protect them from danger.

By 1858, the Conimicut shoal was considered so dangerous that a beacon was erected there to warn vessels of the sunken rocks near the center of the bay between Rocky Point and Bristol. According to *A Brief History of Lifesaving Stations* by Mildred Santille Longo, this early warning device was washed away in 1860, and it was decided in Congress that a more substantial beacon should be erected. In 1868, a beacon or lighthouse built of granite was constructed, and in November of that year it was lighted. In the following year, Mrs. Longo's history tells us that Ferdinand Healey was appointed lightkeeper. As there was no dwelling at the light, it seems that Healey had to make a dangerous one-mile rowboat trip to tend the light.

In 1882, the old granite tower was torn down and the present-day three-story, cast-iron lighthouse was built, with a fifty-eight-foot tower and rooms for a lighthouse keeper and his family. Until 1960, when the Conimicut Light became the last house in the United States to be electrified, the light was powered by kerosene. In 1965, the state deeded the land to the city, which began work in the late 1960s to extend the beach area. By 1966, the lighthouse was fully automated and has continued to be an active U.S. Coast Guard aid to navigation. In the 1980s, a roadway was added, and the park was made easily accessible to all who want to enjoy the bay, whether it be for bathing, fishing or just relaxing and enjoying the fresh sea breezes.

On September 29, 2004, the lighthouse was turned over to the City of Warwick. The Coast Guard still maintained the lighthouse, but the city had the opportunity to make it part of the Conimicut Point Park attraction. As it was difficult for all visitors to get to and view the lighthouse at the site, plans were made to erect a number of kiosks in the park to enable everyone to view the history of the light and its interior via pictures.

The kiosk additions to the already beautiful park would help to make the fourteen-acre site even more popular and attract visitors year-round. Conimicut Point Park is one of Warwick's most treasured summertime recreation areas. Residents and visitors from eight to eighty and beyond can and do come and enjoy this beautiful seaside facility.

Once again, bathers are coming to Conimicut during the summer months to cool off, as these ladies did about 1900. *Donald Skuce Collection (WHS).*

THE CONIMICUT IMPROVEMENT ASSOCIATION

Thanks to many inspired Conimicut residents and sympathetic city administrations over the years, Conimicut has been one of the areas that has undergone a great renaissance since the 1980s. Much of this has been due to the hard work of members of the Conimicut Improvement Association. The association was formed in December 1984 with the goal to improve the social, economic and environmental qualities of life in the village. Many of its goals have been met in partnership with the City of Warwick's Office of Community Development. The village has seen new sidewalks, tree plantings, nineteenth-century street lighting, logo street signs and many other positive accomplishments. Today, Conimicut retains the features that attracted many to ride the trolley line in the early twentieth century and has other newer attractions as well.

HILLSGROVE

The new T.F. Green Airport, recently remodeled, is one of the few airports on the East Coast which is easily accessible for passengers...All major airlines service the airport... An Amtrak rail station will open a mere 1200 feet from the airport, making it the closest rail station to an airport in the country.
—Department of Economic Development

In 1875, when Oliver Payson Fuller wrote his excellent, informative *History of Warwick*, he commented, "To the east of Pontiac, a couple of miles on the Stonington railroad, a thriving little village has sprung up with the past ten years, in connection with the establishment of a new branch of industry." He was referring to Hill's Grove, an area that was then becoming important as the home of the Rhode Island Malleable Iron Works, established by Thomas Jefferson Hill in 1867. Hill purchased about eight hundred acres of land in the vicinity, and his factory employed one hundred hands. During the next century, the village name "Hill's Grove" would be changed to "Hillsgrove," and it would become most famous for the Elizabeth Mill (1875) and the State Airport (1929–31). Today, it is at the center of Warwick's fast-developing industrial area.

THOMAS JEFFERSON HILL

Hill became one of the first of the great "captains of industry" in Rhode Island. His story vividly portrays the spectacular rise of the self-made man. He was born in 1801, the year that Thomas Jefferson became president. His blacksmith father, an admirer of the great Virginian, proudly named his son Thomas

The establishment of the Rhode Island Malleable Iron Works in Hill's Grove heralded the beginnings of the village. *Warwick Historical Society Collection.*

Jefferson Hill and very early tried to instill political ambition in the young boy. In 1846, Thomas Hill became the sole owner of the Providence Machine Shop, the largest and most complete establishment for the manufacture of cotton and woolen machinery in New England. Using the machine shop as a base, Hill was able to expand and extend his fortune and establish a village in Warwick. A village of forty-nine inhabitants had grown up around the Rhode Island Malleable Iron Works, and Hill hired the firm French and MacKenzie to build a number of one-and-a-half-story double homes for the employees of the plant.

RHODE ISLAND MALLEABLE IRON WORKS

Fuller describes the Malleable Iron Works as manufacturing a "multitude of different articles…of all sizes and shapes, from garden rakes and coffee mills to the larger pieces used in connection with cotton and woolen machinery." The original works burned down in August 1918 and was almost immediately rebuilt. The new building was designed by the Providence firm of Jackson, Robertson and Adams and has features patterned after those on Colonial- and Federal-period buildings.

A RAILROAD DEPOT

In addition to the Malleable Iron Works and the company houses, O.P. Fuller tells us that "a short time after the works were started, a tasteful depot was erected, costing about $3000, of which the railway company paid half." The railroad alluded to by Fuller was the Stonington Railroad line, which opened between Providence and Stonington, Connecticut, in 1837.

The railroad line helped Warwick grow during the early nineteenth century by encouraging the development of land adjacent to it. Old areas, such as Apponaug, benefited, and new areas, such as Hillsgrove, became important. The railroad eventually became the New York, Providence and Boston line and then merged into the New York, New Haven and Hartford system in 1893.

When Hill purchased the land in Warwick's central plain, it consisted of little more than woods and flatlands and was not an important part of the early nineteenth-century town. Thanks to Thomas J. Hill, by the late nineteenth century it was a flourishing village with its ironworks, textile mill, a major railroad station, a large school, a lovely church, a company store, fine houses and splendid farmlands and orchards. Much of the growth came when Hill took advantage of the great demand for textiles and mill machinery created by the Civil War. He combined that with the new technical knowledge regarding steam-driven engines. No longer confined to the river for water power, Hill could build on less expensive land and take advantage of the Stonington Railroad to deliver raw materials to his factory and finished products to his customers. The result was the Elizabeth Mill, built in 1875.

Thomas J. Hill realized the importance of the railroad to his industry. This early station was one of the key buildings in the Hill complex. *Henry A.L. Brown Collection (WHS).*

The handsome Elizabeth Mill brought prosperity to the village and provided employment for scores of immigrants in the nineteenth century. *Henry A.L. Brown Collection (WHS).*

THE ELIZABETH MILL

In 1869, Hill, who was then a widower, married Miss Elizabeth C. Kenyon of Warwick. He named the famous Elizabeth Mill in honor of his new wife. Hill built the handsome, large brick structure that still stands at 745 Jefferson Boulevard. Today it is near the center of Warwick's rapidly expanding industrial area. This mill remains a Warwick landmark and has been a Leviton enterprise until recently.

The three-story, brick Elizabeth Mill was a very large mill for its day. It measured 324 by 70 feet and had an extension of 80 by 28 feet added later. One of the building's most recognizable features is the four-story, panel brick tower. Originally, the tower had a mansard roof, which was removed during one of the many renovations and alterations of the mill. During the nineteenth century, the mill employed 265 operatives and had twenty thousand spindles. Its chief manufacture was fine yarn thread. The mill brought a great deal of prosperity to the small village, which grew up earlier around Hill's Rhode Island Malleable Iron Works. It then became necessary to build additional housing behind the mill and along Jefferson Boulevard. Within a short time, a company store under the management of Benjamin C. Sweet was added to the Hill enterprises.

Paternalism in Hillsgrove

In addition to hiring French and MacKenzie to build homes for his workers, Hill paid $4,000 for the construction of a two-story schoolhouse. The second floor of the schoolhouse was used as a hall for religious meetings until 1887, when a new church was built with Hill's financial assistance.

As the very successful industrialist Thomas J. Hill grew older, he turned over much of the actual operation of his mills and foundry to various superintendents and "bosses." One of the most famous of these superintendents was William G. James, who controlled the village during much of the late nineteenth century. Superintendent William G. James was the man most responsible for extending the care and control over the village, and he was the most influential citizen in Hillsgrove for many years.

Control—Economic

Paternalism was profitable for the owners, for in providing housing, entire families could be utilized to work in the mills. Women and children could perform many of the tasks and most often were hired for very low wages. Discipline and control by the factory managers became easy, as the behavior pattern of any one family member reflected on them all. Jobs, housing and general well-being depended on cooperation with the superintendent and mill "bosses." Houses, such as those in the block bounded by Graystone, Thurber, Kilvert and Cottage Streets, could be built and maintained less expensively by the mills than by individuals. Rent for the houses was often deducted from wages, and maintenance crews could be used to repair, paint and build when work at the mill was slow. In addition, workers often found that the company store was the most practical place to purchase their goods, as transportation was difficult and credit at the store was available. The success of the stores meant that a large quantity of food was needed, and in Hillsgrove, a company farm prospered as a result.

Control—Moral

In addition to the economic influence that the company had over the workers by controlling employment, housing and food, many mill owners and superintendents controlled the workers' political, social and, to some degree, moral and religious lives as well. In Hillsgrove, Thomas J. Hill and his superintendent, William G. James, were responsible for the success of a temperance society in the village and for creating a Methodist church, which still stands on Kilvert Street. Hill and his followers were well aware that the church was of prime importance in any mill village. They realized that supporting the local church was a sound investment, as it brought stability and order to the village and fostered a sense of well-being and pride. In addition, the church promoted social activities, as well as meeting the moral and religious needs of its congregation.

THE UNITED METHODIST CHURCH

The United Methodist Church on Kilvert Street traces its origins to 1876, shortly after the Elizabeth Mill was erected. The number of villagers by this time had grown, and many of them met in the schoolhouse that T.J. Hill had erected a few years earlier. The paternalistic mill owner allowed the group to meet on the second floor of the building to conduct services and to organize a "Sabbath School." Villagers in Hill's Grove in the nineteenth century relied on their Sunday schools to provide for their recreational, as well as their spiritual, needs. Among the most cherished memories were those of excursions to Rocky Point. Many church organizations in Rhode Island arranged for a day at the state's most popular resort. Sunday schools were also active during the winter season. There were recitations and singing of carols by the schoolchildren, and then Santa Claus made his appearance. On occasion, sleigh rides were offered for additional enjoyment.

It was eventually realized that in addition to a Sunday school, there was a definite need for a Methodist church building in the village. On May 7, 1884, the Methodist Episcopal Church at Hill's Grove was organized, and George E. Dunbar was appointed its first minister. With the encouragement of the superintendents of the Elizabeth Mill and the Rhode Island Malleable Iron Works, plans were made to build a church. The church building was erected on a lot donated by Thomas J. Hill, who also gave $3,000 toward the cost of the church. His wife, Elizabeth, contributed a great deal to the furnishings for the church, as did the mill superintendent, William G. James. In the 1880s, the $3,000 contribution of Thomas J. Hill seemed like a fortune to the villagers. This was a time when wages were very low, and the amounts of money raised by the congregation were very small in comparison.

In one of the early church fundraisers, a Washington's Birthday supper on February 23, 1899, the cost charged for a meal consisting of "cold meat, brown bread, white bread, doughnuts, cheese, pickles and pies" was twenty cents for adults and ten cents for children. As might be expected, the receipts of a meal such as this rarely raised more than twenty dollars for the church fund. While there was not a great deal of money that exchanged hands at church activities, there was certainly a great opportunity for a good time. Many of the suppers around the turn of the century boasted both good food and excellent music, which was provided by the Hill's Grove Band.

During the difficult times of the Great Depression, the church managed to survive and to grow. Once again, the W.G. James family, so generous in the past, gave additional gifts, and the church was even able to build a parish hall addition and a new parsonage. After World War II, the Hillsgrove United Methodist Church joined the Rhode Island Council of Churches, and by 1959, the church had over three hundred members. Once again, as they had done in the late nineteenth century, the parishioners accepted the challenge of meeting rising costs through a series of activities. The church exists and prospers because of its many parishioners who have often given very unselfishly of both their time and efforts.

To maintain the long traditions established by the church since its inception in the nineteenth century and put forth a truly meaningful religious entity in the twenty-first century proved to be a challenge for the present pastor, Duane Clinker, who came to the Hillsgrove church in 1999. The Reverend Clinker noted that the church was thriving, but many in the congregation felt that maintaining the status quo was not enough. Many of the church elders felt the same way, and in 2005, they decided to "risk everything to either grow in size or start a new congregation to reach out to a larger ministry." The very idea of change meant that the church would never again be the same, and it was difficult to abandon the nice feeling of clinging to old traditions. The decision was made to merge with the Washington Park United Methodist Church. Both church congregations voted unanimously to end the separate existences of the Hillsgrove United Methodist Church and the Washington Park United Methodist Church and create a new entity: the Open Table of Christ. The new church would have one pastor, one budget and multiple sites.

In addition, the Hillsgrove church decided to utilize its major asset, the building on Kilvert Street, and share the building with the Zion Korean United Methodist Church. Once again, tradition gave way to practicality and true spirituality, to the benefit of all involved.

ST. FRANCIS OF ASSISI CHURCH

While the owners and superintendents of the Elizabeth Mill and the Rhode Island Malleable Iron Works supported the Methodist church in the village, they also recognized the need for a Swedish Baptist church and a Roman Catholic church. The Swedish Baptist church no longer exists, but the Saint Francis of Assisi Roman Catholic Church continues to thrive. The Saint Francis of Assisi parish at Hillsgrove includes a school with a large enrollment, a day-care center and a rectory. All are located on Jefferson Boulevard, not far from the former ironworks and Elizabeth Mill. The Swedish Baptist church building, purchased about 1946, is now the rectory for the Catholic church.

During the latter part of the nineteenth century, many Irish and French-Canadian immigrants came to the village to work. In a struggle to maintain their identities in a new environment, many felt the need to cling tenaciously to their native religions and customs. As there was no Catholic church in Hill's Grove before 1900, these Catholic immigrants walked from Hill's Grove to Natick to worship at St. Joseph's Church. By the beginning of the twentieth century, as the demand for workers increased, the number of Catholics in Hill's Grove grew. In 1900, there were enough to call for a mission church in the village.

Missionaries of the Sacred Heart, which had taken charge of St. Joseph's parish in Natick in 1899, sent priests to Hill's Grove weekly to celebrate Mass. The earliest priests celebrated Mass at the public school until May 1900, when the small Mission Church of St. Francis was built. By 1915, Father Francis Van Der Heyden became the priest in charge of the mission at Hillsgrove and remained in that capacity until his death in April 1942. For much of this early period, there was a Mass said in French and one in English to accommodate the major ethnic groups in the village. It was soon found that it was physically impossible to accommodate all of the parishioners in the old frame church at Sunday Mass and on Holy Days, and in addition, many in the parish longed for a school of their own.

VINCENT D'AMORE'S BEAUTIFUL/PRACTICAL COMPLEX

On Easter Sunday 1962, the dream of a new church and a school became a reality when Mass was celebrated in the new St. Francis Church. The church-school complex designed by architect Vincent D'Amore is not only beautiful, but it is extraordinarily practical as well. By attaching the school to the church, D'Amore made it possible for the children to attend church

Recently, the entire village mourned the death of little Michael Marfeo Jr. To keep his memory alive, this playground was built and dedicated.

services without having to face inclement weather. It also allows easy access to the school for special functions of the parish. The school opened in September 1962 with a pre-primary class and four grades. Eight sisters of St. Joseph and two lay teachers staffed it, and at that time, the school had an enrollment of two hundred.

Today, the pastor of St. Francis of Assisi parish is Father Kiley, who is confident that the church will continue to provide the necessary services to Hillsgrove parishioners and to the community as a whole. He sees the proposed railroad station as giving the St. Francis parish the opportunity to offer Sunday Masses to those in transit and to those who stay at the fourteen hotels presently in the area. Today, the St. Francis of Assisi parish serves more than eight hundred families in much the same manner as it has served in Hillsgrove for over one hundred years.

Hillsgrove's Racetrack and Icehouses

One of Warwick's most colorful men in the early twentieth century was J.H. Collingwood, the owner of the Hillsgrove Race Track. Collingwood, in a 1910 interview with a Providence newspaper, noted that he never joined any of the prominent racing associations but was a member of the old "Gentlemen's Driving Club" when, as he put it, "it was a driving club." Collingwood was an active politician in Warwick who, in addition to being sheriff, was a member of the House of Representatives and was the highway commissioner.

Today, the only reminders of the track and Collingwood can be found in the roads named Racing Avenue and Collingwood Street. At one time, however, Collingwood was known to all of Warwick. He was sheriff of Kent County and was involved in the complicated legal maneuvering that followed the failure of the A. & W. Sprague Manufacturing Co. in 1873. The Spragues, one of Rhode Island's wealthiest textile manufacturing families, had assets at the time of over $19 million and outstanding debts of about $14 million. With the Panic of 1873 and the demand for immediate payment, the Spragues could not utilize their assets and went bankrupt. Collingwood felt that his most notable work was in connection with the Sprague failure, as many attachments passed through his hands.

Collingwood made news in 1910 when, at a celebration of his fifty-first wedding anniversary, he clearly came out against Warwick becoming a city at that time. He predicted that "the Valley end of the town might become a city in a couple of years" but "the eastern end of the territory would remain a town." He felt that this was much more sensible than making a city of the whole, as he thought it was against the will of the people and therefore unconstitutional. He clearly recognized that the valley, or westernmost area of Warwick, was highly industrialized and had different needs than the remainder of the town. Within a few years after this interview, Warwick was divided, and the valley area became the town of West Warwick. It has not become a city; but Warwick, the eastern end, did of course in 1931.

Another prominent resident of Hillsgrove who was not directly connected with the mills was George B. Sherwood. He established a large icehouse in the village. An in-depth article on Hillsgrove written in 1903 notes that "a large ice house was erected last fall on the shore of the pond at the northwest corner of the village, and was completely filled with ice." The article goes on to say, "Mr. Sherwood has been very successful during the short time that he has been engaged in business here." During the twentieth century, a number of other businesses, restaurants and recreational enterprises found their way to Hillsgrove.

Hillsgrove

For many decades, this station, now called Sandwich Junction, connected Hillsgrove residents to the outside world and brought workers to the mills. *Warwick Historical Society Collection.*

Thomas Hill's Malleable Iron Works employed many immigrants during the early twentieth century. These workers were given a short break while this photograph was taken. *Dave Matteson Collection.*

THE HILLSGROVE FARM

While the most important aspect of life in Hillsgrove depended on the Thomas Hill enterprises, and these businesses attracted attention, Hillsgrove in the early twentieth century was also famous for its farm. In 1903, the farm was under the care of Edwin A. Gardiner and was considered a model farm. This was the era of paternalism. During this period the farm was an important part of the village and had a great effect on the inhabitants. In 1903, there were about fifty head of cattle on the farm, which distributed most of the milk that was utilized in the mill tenements. In addition to supplying the needs of the village, the farm was also engaged in market gardening and often sent its produce to Providence. Warwick, even in the early twentieth century, was primarily a rural area, and many, like Collingwood, could never imagine the rapid growth that transformed Warwick into Rhode Island's second-largest city.

Hillsgrove was also the home of the tuberculosis hospital or sanatorium during the late nineteenth and early twentieth centuries. Its country-like roads and small population brought patients from the crowded cities to enjoy the "good air" at Hillsgrove.

THE AIRPORT

There were many factors that accounted for the change in Hillsgrove from the small, well-contained village of the early twentieth century to the modern community of today. The most significant single reason often given is the selection of Hillsgrove as the site for the State Airport. The impetus for an airport grew tremendously in 1927, when an attractive young man of twenty-four years, Charles A. Lindbergh, took a $13,000 Ryan monoplane, the *Spirit of St. Louis*, from Roosevelt Field on Long Island, New York, to the Le Bourget Airport in Paris on May 20–21, 1927. This flight, flown alone over thirty-six hundred miles across the Atlantic, made Lindbergh a national hero overnight. Lindbergh, an advocate of commercial aviation, was invited to Rhode Island to spur the demand for an airport in the vicinity of Providence. Lindbergh's efforts resulted in the voters of Rhode Island approving a state airport by 76,281 to 9,369 in the general election of 1928. The main question was not "Should we have an airport?" but "Where should it be?" Early speculation and support came to locate it at Gaspee Point, but eventually Hillsgrove was selected.

The announcement by Harry T. Bodwell, chairman of the State Airport Commission in 1929, that Hillsgrove was to be the site of the new airport was greeted with a great deal of discontent and prompted much criticism of the commission and state government. The site was selected at the recommendation of a New York engineering firm, Black and Bigelow, and time has shown that the decision was based on careful and sensible evaluation.

The *Providence Magazine*, which had supported the cause for aviation for a number of years, was extremely critical of the Hillsgrove choice. In an August 1929 editorial, it charged that

> *despite the recommendation of a survey conducted by impartial aviation and airport engineering experts...despite the recommendation of The Providence Chamber of Commerce...Despite...overwhelming public favor, the State Airport Commission ignored the logical location at Gaspee Point.*

The editorial went on to conclude that "posterity will hardly forgive a failure that is so completely the fault of misdirected reasoning."

Rhode Islanders who had high hopes of seeing a modern airport emerge overnight were sadly disappointed. The state confined its effort in the early period to simply clearing and grading the field. During the early 1930s, the planes landed on grassy strips, as there were no paved runways. Private air companies erected their own hangars, and it wasn't until 1931 that the state began to build a terminal and administration building.

The first decade of flying at the State Airport was often confusing and, in some cases, dangerous. Rhode Island had no laws governing the licensing and operation of aircraft, which meant that an unlicensed plane could engage in interstate flying without any regulation or supervision. In addition, there were no laws governing the erection of buildings in the area, and it was possible that tall buildings or spires within a mile and a half radius of the airport could pose serious problems. One example of this was the steeple of the Hillsgrove Methodist Church. This spire was not removed until 1943, much to the dismay of many of the pilots coming into Hillsgrove.

Senator Green Is Honored

One of the men most responsible for the growth of the airport was Theodore Francis Green. As governor of Rhode Island (1933–37) and then as U.S. senator (1937–61), Green was a constant supporter of aviation. Senator Green was given special recognition for his efforts on both state and national levels. On December 27, 1938, Governor Robert E. Quinn, by executive

Thousands came from all areas of Warwick to witness the dedication of this original airport terminal building in 1931.

order, renamed the State Airport at Hillsgrove "the Theodore Francis Green State Airport of Rhode Island."

The growth from this point on was phenomenal. A hangar built in 1938 to handle anticipated needs for ten years was filled to capacity by the end of 1940. During that year, the Green Airport was cited as being the seventh-busiest facility in the nation. In 1940, a Uniform Aeronautical Regulatory Act made federal registration for all aircraft and pilot's licenses mandatory.

The Theodore Francis Green Airport at Hillsgrove has served the state in both peace and war. After being used by the federal government as an army air force base, the facility was returned to the state in 1945. Since that time, Hillsgrove has been the site of one of the more important airports along the East Coast. It has continued to play a part in the overall defense plan—since 1948, the airport has handled various aspects of the Air National Guard (152nd Fighter Bomber Squadron).

Over the last seventy-eight years, there have been a number of significant periods of expansion. One of the periods of greatest growth came in the 1950s. Between 1953 and 1957, the number of passengers using the facility rose by 100,000, and in the following year, it increased again by 16.2 percent. By 1957, the Green Airport was one of only sixty-four airports in the United States that serviced more than 100,000 passengers. Much of the ability to enplane, or handle, the increased numbers was made possible by voter approval of a bond issue of $1.5 million in 1956. This bond issue provided for the building of a new terminal at the State Airport, which was dedicated in 1961.

By the 1960s, the jet age had arrived, and once again the Theodore F. Green Airport sought to expand to utilize the advanced technology and to compete with larger airports. By March 1966, the runways were able to provide the necessary space for landing the large jets that were becoming the modern vehicles for flying.

Of great significance was the completion of the "airport connector" between Interstate Route 95 and the airport. This two-mile road made it possible for rapid transportation from all areas of Rhode Island, as the Hillsgrove Airport is located near the geographical center of Rhode Island. The advertising for the event laid claim to the ability to reach Providence from Theodore Francis Green Airport via Route I-95 in fifteen minutes.

The next twenty years witnessed phenomenal growth in the number of planes and passengers coming into Green. In the year 1986, T.F. Green was one of the fastest-growing airports in the country. In January 1992, Governor Bruce Sundlun inaugurated a plan that led to a two-tier airport terminal with fifteen gates, which could accommodate three million passengers annually. This became a reality in 1995. Those who were used to the small airport were pleasantly surprised by the beauty and scope of the new terminal.

Today, Hillsgrove is home to one of the finest modern airports in New England. It is serviced by all major airlines, providing millions of passengers with flights to many major U.S. cities.

All Warwick residents were not in favor of the recent airport expansion, however. There was great fear that there would be much more noise and traffic that would alter the quality of life in the neighborhood. This has been true, of course, but most observers of the airport have agreed that the expansion has been a success and that the airport at Hillsgrove now houses excellent facilities. Obviously, there are many problems to be worked on, in addition to noise, fumes and parking. Today, more people are flying out of T.F. Green than at any other time in its history, and Hillsgrove has been affected to a great extent by the expansion.

THE INDUSTRIAL PARK

The great changes that befell the village of Hillsgrove with the building of the State Airport were matched by those brought about by the tremendous impact of industrialization along Jefferson Boulevard. Modern industry came to Hillsgrove for many of the same reasons that prompted Thomas Jefferson Hill to build his Rhode Island Malleable Iron Works and Elizabeth Mill there. Hill found the "Plains," as the region was once called, underdeveloped and the land reasonably priced. City planners in the mid-twentieth century saw the same advantages.

The farsighted T.J. Hill knew that the railroad would go through the area and that it would stop for freight, giving him easy access to the markets he needed for his goods. In the same manner, Warwick's city administrators knew that I-95 was coming through Hillsgrove and that there would be access ramps to Jefferson Boulevard, providing the section with a main artery to customers all along the interstate highway. Today, with the proposed railroad stop at the airport, Hillsgrove will be even more readily accessible to the rest of New England and the country. In T.J. Hill's era, and in modern times, Warwick officials viewed the coming of industry as a boon for the town and a relief to taxpayers. Some of the past still remains.

Despite the very rapid growth and the changes that occurred in Hillsgrove in the last half of the twentieth century, surprisingly enough, the basic mill and mill village are still visually evident. The airport has, of course, greatly altered Post Road, but along Greystone, Thurber, Kilvert and Cottage Streets, as well as part of Jefferson Boulevard, mill houses still exist and remind us of the village that once stood there. One of the reasons that so much of Hillsgrove has remained so intact until the close of the century is because the Elizabeth Mill sold its mill houses to citizens in the area in 1926, when it ceased operations as a textile mill. Once the workers acquired the property, they were able to maintain and modernize the houses to meet their needs. Some of these houses, such as those on Greystone Street, were built in 1867 by the firm French and MacKenzie, which was noted for its Greek Revival–style dwellings. Many of these houses have not only survived, but have also been turned into excellent modern homes. Some of the newer ones, located mostly in the area called "Dogtown," had dormer windows on the second floor. There were duplex outhouses to the rear of the house, and there was a common well halfway between each house. When the Elizabeth Mill closed and sold its houses to individuals in 1926, there was no electricity or indoor plumbing. Once the houses were privately owned, significant changes were often made. One of the first was usually to utilize the long pantry in each house to put in a modern bathroom. In many others, owners built porches and additional rooms and added various modifications, depending on individual tastes and needs.

One of these homes at 878 Jefferson Boulevard was owned by the late Joseph and Violet McKeon. Joseph McKeon, who was a science teacher and supervisor in the Warwick school system, had lived in the house for most of his life. When speaking of the 1930s, McKeon remembered, "The kitchen was the only room with plenty of heat. We had an old black stove and had to heat our water on it." McKeon added that to save on heat, "we closed off rooms in the winter to keep warm."

Like so many others who still live in the village today, the McKeons worked in either the Elizabeth Mill or the Rhode Island Malleable Iron Works. Joe's mother, Mary Louise Lafleur McKeon, worked in the Elizabeth Mill when she was only nine years old. Child labor laws in Rhode Island's mills either were nonexistent or were not adhered to.

When Joe McKeon was a boy delivering papers in the village, common usage divided Hillsgrove into three sections called "Foundry Village," "Mill Village" and "Dogtown" (as there were so many families that had dogs there). The airport didn't exist then, and the area consisted of a great deal of woods and swamps. In a 1992 interview, McKeon noted that "there was nothing more than a winding horse path through woods from the pond near Wethersfield Commons' entrance today to the Greenwood Inn." McKeon also remembered the way that Jefferson Boulevard looked before the maple trees were taken down to widen the road. Thomas Jefferson Hill had planted these trees along each side of the dirt road that passed through the village and past the mill. The road was called Jefferson Avenue then, and because of the trees, the village was called Hill's Grove. Pleasant memories of swimming in "Pitsey's Pond," going to Norden's strawberry patch (now Strawberry Field

Road) and playing baseball in the field across from the mill were matched by remembrances of the tyranny of the factory whistle in the foundry. Whistles indicated when to arrive at work, when to start, when to go to lunch and when to stop working.

LIFE IN THE FOUNDRY

Work at the ironworks was often strenuous and dangerous. Most of the workers in the early period were happy to work there, however, and to enjoy the paternalistic role played by Hill and his superintendents. In a 1992 interview, the late Joseph McKeon, who had lived in the village all his life, recalled working a twelve-hour day in the foundry for thirty cents an hour. He learned to understand what his father, Andrew, who was a "moulder" at the foundry and made all the samples by hand, meant when he said, "There isn't a good job in the foundry. Even Mr. Block, the chemist, has to get up at 4:00 a.m." In the foundry, the whistle also blew at "heat time" to let the workers know that the iron was ready. The iron, which began heating at 4:00 a.m. when the chemist arrived, was usually ready at 3:30 p.m. At the sound of the whistle, the unskilled workers lined

Work in the foundry in the early years was both arduous and dangerous. These workers toiled long hours, often with little compensation. *David Matteson Collection (WHS).*

up for one of the most difficult tasks in the foundry. As the molten metal came out of the furnace, the workers had to "catch it" with their large ladles while the iron was hot. Next they would "carry the iron" to where they would be instructed to pour it into molds. These men were on "piece work" and received five cents for each ladle they carried and poured into the molds. Burns were common, and the difficult work would continue at a steady pace until all the iron for that day was used. This practice was prevalent in the old 1867 mill, which burned down, and in the 1918 mill, which replaced it.

During the Depression years of the 1930s, the competition for employment was so great that often men were selected on the basis of their athletic prowess, as the Rhode Island Malleable Iron Works was very fond of its baseball team. An important part of village life was playing baseball at the field across from the mill. Jobs were scarce during the 1930s, and McKeon felt that one of the reasons he was hired by Rhode Island Malleable Iron Works was that he could play on its team. Later, when McKeon was hired to teach science at Lockwood, this experience helped. All male teachers were expected to perform extracurricular duties, usually in coaching, and Joe served as the assistant baseball coach.

Greenwood Inn

During Prohibition, Hillsgrove was known for its speakeasies. One of the most well known was the Greenwood Inn at the end of Jefferson Boulevard. The inn had once been a stagecoach stop and then an important railroad station when the Stonington Railroad opened in 1837. Eighty years later, the Greenwood Inn was again attracting customers. Those who remember the time recall that it was a saloon, with no restaurant, and that it was infamous for its fights and rowdy crowds. One of the positive changes in Hillsgrove occurred when Henry and Norma Papa purchased the Greenwood Inn in 1951 and made it a fine family restaurant.

St. Joseph's Hospital Annex

Because Hillsgrove was still considered "out in the country," it was selected as the site for St. Joseph's Hospital Annex. This facility was located at the end of Blackburn Street and was inaugurated to help victims of tuberculosis, a dreaded killer in the early twentieth century.

Living in Hillsgrove had a number of advantages; one was the proximity of Sholes Roller Skating Rink. Many a local romance began here. *Warwick Historical Society Collection.*

SHOLES RINK

In the 1930s, Hillsgrove was also becoming well known as a center of entertainment at the Hillsgrove Country Club, where the Sholes Skating Rink was located at the time. There was dancing every Wednesday and Saturday night to Harold Sheffer's Hillsgrove Orchestra, and in addition, there were floor shows and dining facilities. Golf was beginning to come into its own, and a nine-hole "pitch and putt" golf course was added, as well as a practice driving range.

THE BOURDON AIRCRAFT COMPANY AND HOLLAND BREW

After the Elizabeth Mill closed its doors in 1936, the Bourdon Aircraft Company used part of the mills for the manufacture of airplanes, but with only limited success. After the repeal of Prohibition, the premises housed the Consumers Brewing Company, which made Holland Brew, a domestic beer. The beer company gave tours of the brewery, which were popular—at the end of the tour, visitors were invited to sample the company's product.

The All-Important Interstate Highways

In 1960, all of Warwick knew that Interstate Route 95 would go through the city and that Warwick would have a number of exit ramps from the new highway. This, of course, meant that industry would be attracted to the Hillsgrove section of the city, and in 1960, Leesona moved onto Strawberry Field Road and Spiedel Corporation and the Mays Manufacturing Company moved into Hillsgrove. This expansion of the industrial base, and the later growth of industry on Jefferson Boulevard, gave Warwick the expanded tax base it desperately needed.

The year 1964 proved to be a most significant year, as proposals for an east–west link connecting Warwick and Cranston (Route 37) became a reality. Route I-95 was connected to the link in 1965, and shortly thereafter, I-95 was linked to Jefferson Boulevard. This further aided the industrial expansion.

Also in 1964, after decades of debate, ground was broken for a fifty-acre sewage treatment plant that was put into operation off Service Road in Hillsgrove in 1965. Large-scale industrial expansion had become a reality. While this was hailed positively by many in the city, the residents of Hillsgrove became concerned as they witnessed the beginning of the end of a lifestyle with which they had grown comfortable over the years.

Now all that remains of the old foundry that launched the village is this façade, to the left of the Valet Parking Sign. It was kept intact when the modern hotel was built next to it.

Today, much of the area in Hillsgrove is becoming part of the Metro Center Plaza, which will include a railroad station and several hotels and apartment complexes. The attempt is being made to build a depot in Hillsgrove that would be truly modern and in keeping with the improvements in rail travel for the twenty-first century. The old Rhode Island Malleable Iron Works is close to the center of the proposed $55 million development.

When it became known that a new station would be built in Warwick to bring passengers to the T.F. Green Airport by rail, it became obvious to many that additional hotel accommodations would be needed in Hillsgrove. Once again, the Malleable Iron Works became the center of attention. Joseph Piscopio, owner of the Jefferson Grille, decided that the four-acre site of the former ironworks would be ideal for the erection of a 163-room hotel and a 110-unit apartment complex. This Hilton Garden Inn will be part of the Metro Center Plaza in Warwick's new Station District. Hillsgrove Village, as it was in the nineteenth century, is a vital part of Warwick's growth and heritage.

PAWTUXET

Today's Pawtuxet Village…nestled between bustling communities and commercial areas [is where] *some of Rhode Island's most prominent historical sites can be found. Whether walking along historic Post road or strolling through Pawtuxet Park, visitors will easily feel the Village's sense of pride.*
—*Hazel Kennedy and Scott Avedisian,* The Walking Tour of Historic Pawtuxet Village, *1999*

Pawtuxet is one of the most attractive villages in New England. It is unique in the fact that one section of the village is in Cranston and the other in Warwick. Unlike other Warwick villages, Pawtuxet is situated in an area removed from the nineteenth-century mill sites and twentieth-century major arteries of trade and traffic. Thanks to its location and a number of historically minded citizens, much of Pawtuxet exudes the charm and serenity of an early nineteenth-century village, with a number of fine colonial dwellings and significant historical sites. The picturesque sign at the bridge today, which simply states "Pawtuxet River—one of the bounds of Providence mentioned in the Indian deed," depicts a rather pleasant scene of Roger Williams being greeted by the Indians. The history surrounding the early seventeenth-century settlement, however, tells us that the early years were far from serene. From the beginning of its long history, Pawtuxet was rife with controversy, deceit, forgery and even treason.

Controversy over the ownership of the land and the extent of the deed prompted a lifelong bitterness between the colony's founder, Roger Williams, and William Harris, one of the first settlers. The history of the village was also greatly affected by the animosity between Pawtuxet's leading

This charming scene shows the bridge over the river near the falls that connects the two sections of Pawtuxet Village. *Warwick Historical Society Collection.*

citizen, William Arnold, and Warwick's founder, Samuel Gorton. As the bitterness developed, Samuel Gorton moved into the area near the falls, and the Pawtuxet colonists, many of whom had come to the area to escape from the harsh rule of the Puritans in Boston, actually asked to be placed under Massachusetts jurisdiction to stop Gorton from settling there. This decision by the Pawtuxet men has prompted many historians to question the reasons and motives of such a drastic action. The Pawtuxet defection to Massachusetts, in addition to causing hardship to Gorton and his followers, was probably the main reason that Roger Williams changed his original land policies and obtained a charter in 1644.

A number of noted historians, including Samuel Greene Arnold, O.P. Fuller and Sidney S. Rider, have attempted to gather the facts from early colonial records in order to explain the controversies and to evaluate the significance of the events. One of the major historians at the turn of the century, Sidney S. Rider, in 1904 charged that the original deed confirming Roger Williams's purchase of the land from the Indians, dated 1638, was altered by William Harris and William Arnold in an attempt to extend their landholdings.

Pawtuxet

The Early Settlers

The first four settlers in Pawtuxet in 1638, according to nineteenth-century historian Samuel Greene Arnold, were William Harris, William Arnold, William Carpenter and Zachary Rhodes. They settled in the area close to Pawtuxet Falls. The leader and patriarch of the early settlement was William Arnold, the oldest and wealthiest of the original thirteen purchasers of the Providence Plantations. Carpenter and Rhodes were his sons-in-law. William Carpenter had married Elizabeth, the elder daughter of William Arnold, and he, along with his father-in-law, was one of the Pawtuxet purchasers. Zachary Rhodes married Joanne, another of William Arnold's daughters, and very early moved to Pawtuxet.

In addition, William's two sons, Benedict and Stephen Arnold, joined the rest of the family in the area. Benedict Arnold quickly developed great skill in mastering the Indian languages and aided his father in establishing a trading post near the falls in Pawtuxet. Stephen Arnold and Zachary Rhodes are credited with building the first gristmill there and laying out "Arnold's Road" (Broad Street) northward to meet the Old Pequot Path.

Differences between Roger Williams and the Harris-Arnold factions concerning land ownership policies became very obvious—the twelve purchasers wanted the Pawtuxet lands listed separately. This was so that newcomers would not get a portion of this territory as they had with the Providence lands. As events unfolded, the disagreements became more acute, as Harris, Arnold and Carpenter acquired more lands in Pawtuxet from the other proprietors. As early as July 27, 1640, attempts were made to draw a boundary line dividing Providence from Pawtuxet. One of the reasons was fear that undesirable settlers might come to Providence and assume control of the government, thereby diminishing the role of the thirteen original purchasers and jeopardizing their land claims. The most feared of these recent arrivals was Samuel Gorton.

By September 1643, Massachusetts ordered Gorton to appear before the general court of that colony. Gorton and his followers refused to surrender, and there was a siege that lasted several days. Gorton and his men, recognizing the hopelessness of their situation, agreed to articles of surrender to go as "freemen and neighbors" to Boston. Instead, they were treated as captives and placed in jail. Eventually, thanks to the Earl of Warwick, Gorton was able to have his claims recognized by England. In gratitude to the earl, the colony was named Warwick in his honor.

While the founding fathers of Rhode Island were often engrossed in problems of religion, politics and land deeds, the village of Pawtuxet began to grow. Horace Belcher, veteran Rhode Island newspaperman and an excellent source for Pawtuxet materials, made a careful study of the early accounts of Pawtuxet before King Philip's War. He places a great deal of emphasis on the early settlements, a trading post and the gristmill near the falls.

King Philip's War

The struggle of the early settlers to establish a thriving village in the wilderness along the banks of the Pawtuxet River was hampered by many obstacles during the first four decades. Bitter quarrels over religion, politics and land kept the Harris, Arnold and Carpenter families in nearly constant turmoil with their neighbors in Providence and Warwick. In 1676, the village was burned to the ground by the Indians during King Philip's War. Not only were houses burned, livestock stolen and years of hard work demolished, but a number of lives were lost as well.

Before Pawtuxet fell to the wrath of the Indians, however, a great deal of progress had been made, and after the Indian danger diminished, Pawtuxet was able to emerge as a thriving village. The meadows had proven to be very productive. In the 1670s, William Carpenter's farm at Bellefonte, along the banks of the Pawtuxet River, was large and thriving, with a sizeable flock of sheep, a herd of cattle and fifteen horses. His son Joseph, along with Zachariah Rhodes and Stephen Arnold, had established a successful gristmill at Pawtuxet Falls and had cut a road through the wilderness that helped bring trade and prosperity to the small village. In 1659, the first settlers, William Arnold, William Carpenter and William Harris, removed themselves from Massachusetts's jurisdiction and believed they had established a valid claim to nearly one-third of the area of present-day Rhode Island. All three of these founders lived through King Philip's War, and all died believing that their land claims were successful.

In 1696, the Pawtuxet River was determined as the boundary between Warwick and Providence, and by 1714, the final boundaries of the Pawtuxet Purchase were settled. In 1754, Cranston was separated from Providence, and Pawtuxet north of the river became part of the newly created town.

The era that began when William and Mary ascended to the throne in England marked the time that Warwick, like all of Rhode Island, came into its own in agriculture and trade. Warwick was able to overcome its internal problems, settling its western border with Connecticut and satisfactorily ending the Pawtuxet claims. The colony also became a significant part of the ever-growing sea trade. Much of the latter was due to the leadership

The Pawtuxet River marked the boundary of Providence in the early deed. Merchant John Brown's marker let friends know that his Warwick estate was five miles from the bridge. *Warwick Historical Society Collection.*

of Major John Greene Jr. During his tenure as deputy governor, the town of Warwick was nearly destroyed by a smallpox epidemic in 1690–91, witnessed the introduction of paper money as bills of credit and welcomed the beginnings of a post office. Major Greene is also regarded as a champion of Rhode Island rights and especially as the man who introduced Rhode Island to the controversial practice of using privateers. While England was at war for over thirty years in the 1690–1763 period, there was a demand that merchant ships arm themselves to make war on the mother country's enemies. As an incentive, ships receiving privateer commissions were allowed to keep nine-tenths of the spoils of war. Pawtuxet's inclination for the sea became obvious quite early.

Low prices for agricultural products and the difficulty of acquiring and clearing land made it easy for young men to be lured from their farms to seek adventure and high profits as privateers. Historian Samuel Greene Arnold tells us that eighty-four vessels of all sizes were built in the colony and were manned by native seamen. A number of these ships were built in the shipyards at Apponaug and Pawtuxet.

Vessels such as these were called "double enders." They brought seamen from Pawtuxet to Block Island and all along the Atlantic Coast. *Warwick Historical Society Collection.*

The role played by privateers, however, was only one of the segments of the lucrative maritime enterprises that were to aid in Pawtuxet's growth as a seaport town. In 1712, many of the restrictions placed on the American colonies in regard to the slave trade were removed. When the Treaty of Utrecht (1713), which concluded Queen Anne's War, gave England the right to furnish Spanish America with 144,000 slaves over a thirty-year period, the colonies were encouraged to participate in this lucrative trade.

The key to the maritime prosperity was the trade with the West Indies, which brought sugar and molasses into the colony. These were distilled into rum, a commodity accepted nearly everywhere and by no means confined to the African trade. The distilling of rum reached a high point in the middle years of the eighteenth century and was another important aspect of life in Pawtuxet. The operation of a still house had its own peculiar problems, and we have the story of the death of Dr. Zuriel Waterman to attest to these. In a statement from George Waterman, we learn that on September 20, 1786:

> *Joseph Rhodes Senior descended a Cistern in the distill House to discharge a quantity of Putrid stagnated water;...as soon as he arrived to the bottom, he* [said] *"how dreadfully it smells here, I feel faint!" He fell immediately.*

Zachariah Rhodes and Zuriel Waterman went into the vat to help the stricken man, and they were both overcome by the fumes. Zachariah survived, but Joseph Rhodes and Zuriel Waterman suffocated.

Internal Improvements and Calamities

During the first thirty years of the eighteenth century, Warwick's population increased dramatically. As the population grew, so did the demand for internal improvements on roads and bridges. As late as 1704, there was no bridge across the Pawtuxet River leading into Warwick. The crossing was at a ford, or "Indian wading place," a short distance below the Pawtuxet side of the present-day Warwick Avenue Bridge. Once wagons and other wheeled vehicles came into greater use, serious problems arose, as there were times following excessive rains when the water reached such a height that to ford it was impractical. On May 2, 1711, a bridge was built leading into the Warwick side of the village of Pawtuxet. This was but the first of many, as floods often wiped out the earlier structures, including a covered

Fire was often a threat to the early Pawtuxet schools. This building withstood the test of time, and most village children learned their ABCs here. *Madeline Toy Collection (WHS).*

bridge named for Ephraim Bowen, a local Pawtuxet hero. Natural calamities also had their effect on the town. In February 1759, a great flood caused a considerable amount of damage in Pawtuxet when the south end of the Pawtuxet Bridge was nearly destroyed. In addition, the village witnessed two earthquake shocks in the spring and a major nor'easter in the winter of 1761. During 1761–62, when so many disastrous fires occurred, the colony's old fire laws were amended.

SMUGGLING

Almost from the beginning of the century, Rhode Island won a reputation for contrariness, as well as for illegal trading and piracy. This increased after 1733, when the tax called the Molasses Act was passed. The trade in rum, made from molasses, was so lucrative that Warwick ship captains and owners, like most of the others in New England, found that it was more profitable to smuggle than to comply with the law. The many coves and inlets in Warwick, especially those around Warwick Cove, Mill Pond Cove and Pawtuxet, made smuggling relatively easy. Nearly all of Pawtuxet's inhabitants benefited from the increased trade. Those directly concerned with ships and supplies were obvious beneficiaries. In addition, farmers received higher prices, and artisans found a market for their talents as Warwick began supplying the major ports of Newport and Providence. During the later part of the eighteenth century, Pawtuxet and Apponaug became very active and significant ports in Narragansett Bay. By this period, more ships were leaving Warwick for far-flung ports as the triangular trade between Rhode Island, the West Indies and Africa increased.

As might be expected, there were also great profits and dangers involved in using rum to purchase African natives for the nefarious slave trade. One house that is still standing as a reminder of the part Pawtuxet captains played in this trade is the Captain Thomas Remington House at 47–49 Post Road in the Pawtuxet section of Warwick. Many old-time Pawtuxet residents say that they can remember when there were still chains and shackles in the basement of this fine 1740 Colonial house.

The maritime activities of Warwick's sailors were not confined to the triangular trade exclusively, for there was also fishing, whaling and the coastal trade. Without doubt, however, the lucrative profits made from the triangular trade dominated, and any attempt by England to curtail the trade with the West Indies resulted in opposition. Warwick, with its coves and inlets, joined the rest of the colony in smuggling activities after the mother country passed the 1708 Acts of Trade and the 1733 Molasses Act, both of which placed taxes on goods coming in from the West Indies and diminished the colonists' profit.

The French and Indian War

The French and Indian War witnessed the colony engaging in illegal trade with the enemy. An embargo had been passed on trade with the West Indies, but Rhode Island repeatedly violated this and continued to trade with the French and Spanish colonies.

It was during this war that a large number of Pawtuxet men sailed on privateers. While the profits were great, so, too, were the dangers. Over 130 ships from Narragansett ports were "taken, plundered, cast away, and lost at sea" from 1756 to 1763, and Pawtuxet sailors were among the casualties.

By February 1763, the French and Indian War was over. The Peace of Paris was signed, ending what historians have called "the most wide-spread, costly, and sanguinary strife which the world had ever seen." Within a short time, the cost of the war and the fruits of the victory proved to be the wedge that would separate the American colonists from England. Pawtuxet played a significant role in this struggle.

The *Gaspee* Incident

Much like other seacoast towns, residents of Pawtuxet felt that England, in its zeal to enforce its trade laws, threatened to destroy their trade and usurped their rights as Englishmen. It was near Pawtuxet where the most serious of the early protests against the British took place. This was the burning of the British revenue schooner *Gaspee* in June 1772.

Relations between the British patrols in Narragansett Bay and the colonists had reached a new low point after 1763, when British admiral John Montagu selected Lieutenant William Dudingston, captain of the *Gaspee*, to patrol the waters of Narragansett Bay. Captain Dudingston became infamous for harassing small sloops in Rhode Island waters. Most Rhode Islanders felt that he had violated their rights as Englishmen, and Dudingston was one of the most despised British captains in New England. On June 8, 1772, a Providence sloop, *Hannah*, owned by John Brown and under the captaincy of Benjamin Lindsey, left Newport Harbor for Providence. It was approached by the *Gaspee*, which attempted to overhaul it. Captain Lindsey had no intention of submitting to a search when it was possible to outwit Dudingston and outsail the *Gaspee*. Lindsey quickly began to outrun the larger British vessel. Besides the advantage of speed, the Providence vessel was of a "lighter draft" and could sail in shallow water. Lindsey realized that the *Gaspee* was recklessly chasing him, and at Namquit Point, since known as Gaspee Point, Captain Lindsey turned the *Hannah* sharply to the west, seemingly to elude the *Gaspee*. Lindsey warily avoided shoal water and lured the larger vessel into a sandbar, where it ran hard aground.

AN EYEWITNESS ACCOUNT OF THE BURNING

Fortunately, Ephraim Bowen, who later became one of Pawtuxet's leading citizens and who took part in the burning of the *Gaspee*, has given us an eyewitness account of the events that took place during that historic action. Bowen did not write of the stirring events, however, until August 1839, after more than sixty-seven years had passed. Bowen, despite his eighty-six years of age, had excellent recall, and his story, sharpened by frequent repetition, is accurate in almost every detail.

According to Bowen, Lindsey "arrived at Providence about sunset, when he immediately informed Mr. John Brown, one of our first and most respectable merchants, of the situation of the *Gaspee*." Brown quickly realized that this was an opportunity to destroy the British revenue schooner and issued a call for all who wished to join him in the move against the *Gaspee*. Historian Horace Belcher believes that "there is good evidence that at least one boat came from Pawtuxet." Captain Abraham Whipple, who led the party, carefully approached the *Gaspee*. Dudingston was summoned on deck by his sentries and asked, "Who comes there?" Whipple is said to have answered, "I want to come onboard." Dudingston responded, "Stand off, you can't come onboard." Whipple then is alleged to have said words to the effect of, "I am the sheriff of the county of Kent. I am come for the commander of this vessel, and have him I will, dead or alive; men, spring to your oars!"

Bowen, in his narrative, recalls:

> *As soon as Dudingston began to hail, Joseph Bucklin, who was standing by the main thwart, by my right side, said to me, "Eph, reach me your gun, and I can kill that fellow." I reached it to him, accordingly; when, during Capt. Whipple's replying, Bucklin fired and Dudingston fell; and Bucklin exclaimed, "I have killed the rascal."*

One of the most significant episodes in the history of the village revolves around the taking of British prisoners from the *Gaspee* to the Rhodes still house.

Very quickly, we are told, "in less time than a minute after Capt. Whipple's answer," the boats were alongside the British revenue schooner and men boarded it without opposition.

Dudingston fell to the deck with wounds in the groin and arm. Dr. John Mawney, who also participated in the event, hastened to the cabin and tended to Dudingston's wounds. Shortly after Dudingston was cared for, the crew of the *Gaspee* was taken from the vessel. Bowen, who was very familiar with Pawtuxet, tells us that they "landed Dudingston at the old Stillhouse Wharf at Pawtuxet, and put the chief into the house of Joseph Rhodes."

The significance of the defiance of Rhode Islanders in 1772 extended beyond the isolated incident of June 9. The news of the burning spread from Rhode Island to the rest of the colonies. Many openly applauded this "first act of violence" and made preparations for assistance should the British react with force. Committees of Correspondence, the forerunner of the Continental Congress, were organized as a result.

The Pawtuxet Armory was given by the state to the Pawtuxet Rangers out of gratitude for their loyalty during the Dorr Rebellion. *Warwick Historical Society Collection.*

THE PAWTUXET RANGERS

Sensing that open hostilities were imminent, the men of Pawtuxet, on October 29, 1774, obtained a charter from the Rhode Island Assembly and organized the Pawtuxet Rangers. The militiamen elected Samuel Aborn as their captain. Two years earlier, Aborn, in his small sloop *Sally*, had taken the anchors, guns, stores and other effects from the *Gaspee* to Pawtuxet. Benjamin and Rhodes Arnold were lieutenants in the Pawtuxet Rangers, and Stephen Greene was elected to the position of ensign. Horace Belcher tells us that "at least half the membership bore the family names Aborn, Arnold, Rhodes and Smith."

Victory and independence did not come easily. The eight long years between the outbreak of hostilities in 1775 and the final victory in 1783 meant a great deal of suffering and hardship for Warwick. With the exception of three battles, Rhode Island troops fought in every major action of the war.

The Continental Navy

While this was happening, in December 1775 the Continental Congress created a Continental navy, and Rhode Islander Esek Hopkins was appointed as commander in chief. A number of seamen familiar with Warwick ports were given commands. Among these, Abraham Whipple and John B. Hopkins were named as captains, and Rhodes Arnold of Pawtuxet was commissioned as a first lieutenant. As nearly all Warwick men had some experience with the sea, many volunteered to serve with Whipple and Hopkins in the fledgling Continental navy. Many Pawtuxet men, however, preferred the more lucrative service of "privateering" more than service in the Continental navy. This method of warfare, regarded by many as legalized piracy, had long been a favored enterprise in the colony. John Brown of Providence became famous, if not notorious, for his part, and Warwick's Greene, Rhodes and Aborn families played leading roles.

While Rhode Island was busily engaged in building defenses and celebrating the victories of Esek Hopkins's voyage to Nassau, the bay was temporarily free of British ships. Realizing this, Rhode Island chose this time to issue what is generally regarded as the Rhode Island Declaration of Independence on May 4, 1776. This came two months before the general declaration of the united colonies.

For a short while in the spring of 1776, the calamities of war seemed to be balanced by good fortune in Rhode Island. It was not uncommon in many Warwick families to see father and son, uncles and even grandfathers taking some part in the military actions of the period. In Pawtuxet and Warwick, this was especially true of the Greene, Arnold and Rhodes families.

On December 3, the British entered Rhode Island waters with seven ships of the line, four frigates and seventy transports, with six thousand troops onboard. On December 8, 1776, the king's army landed in Middletown and, Rhode Island historian S.G. Arnold tells us, "after a night of pillage, the next morning marched into Newport." Within a few days, officials in neighboring Massachusetts and Connecticut, realizing the danger to the mainland of Rhode Island and to their states, sent help to contain the British in Newport. Some of these neighboring troops were assigned to defend the fort at Pawtuxet Neck.

Warwick's Forts

In 1775, the British naval commander in Narragansett Bay, Captain James Wallace, brought fear to the hearts of the residents of Warwick and

Samuel Aborn played a key role on both land and sea during the Revolutionary War. As host of the Golden Ball Inn, he was instrumental in promoting the spirit of independence in the village. *Warwick Historical Society Collection.*

Providence. Wallace threatened an attack on Providence and sent a fleet to the upper part of Narragansett Bay. He stopped near Conimicut Point and pillaged the area around Warwick Neck, stealing a large number of livestock. Shortly after this, in October, Wallace ordered the bombardment of Bristol. Following this, the fort at Pawtuxet was built on land owned by Captain Thomas Remington and was hastily manned with a company of fifty men.

The fort at Pawtuxet was manned by the Pawtuxet Rangers, officially ranked in the state militia as the Second Independent Company of the County of Kent, which at that time numbered fifty and was led by Captain Samuel Aborn, First Lieutenant Benjamin Arnold, Second Lieutenant Rhodes Arnold and Ensign Stephen Greene, all of Pawtuxet. The commander of the militia unit was Samuel Aborn, one of the leading citizens of the village and the "host at the Golden Ball Inn, on Post Road, at the western end of the village." Aborn remained the rangers' commander throughout the struggle for independence.

Aborn's experiences during the war serve to remind us of the bitterness and the tragedy of the time. Very early in the struggle, his sloop, *Sally*, was captured by the British, causing him serious financial hardship. Later, his young son, a boy of fourteen, joined the Continental army. Boys at that young age were anxious to take part in the war and often served as drummer boys. Young Aborn, at the special request of General Nathanael Greene, was granted permission to return home because of ill health. Belcher tells us that it was too late, as "the boy came home only to die."

The fort, with its small watch house, became the responsibility of the rangers, who not only took part in building it, but also manned it during the early months of 1777. The rangers at this time were little more than armed villagers, as each man furnished his own musket and equipment. Officers studied military drill and tactics and provided additional supplies and equipment. Most of the rangers carried out their business in the village, subject to call when needed. At this time, real estate value in Warwick sank at least 25 percent, and according to W.A. Greene, "since the blockade it had cost the inhabitants to live, on an average, three shillings per week more than their earnings."

The Saratoga Guns

It was during 1777, called "the time of mixed fortunes" and the "year of miracles," that the British had planned a three-pronged attack to cut the colonies in half along the line of Lake Champlain and the Hudson Valley. Three British armies were to meet at Albany and present an unmatched force that would have devastated the Continental army. Fortunately for the American cause, poor communications and a series of blunders made this impossible. As a result, only the army under General John Burgoyne met the Americans at Saratoga, not far from Albany.

General Washington had sent many of his best troops to Saratoga to aid General Horatio Gates and his second in command, General Benedict Arnold. In addition, militia units from all over New England, possibly including the Pawtuxet Rangers, swelled the American ranks. Burgoyne ordered an attack on the Americans on October 7, 1777. He advanced with fifteen hundred men and six pieces of artillery. The British might have been successful, but Arnold, without orders and in defiance of Gates (whom many believed was about to call for a retreat), pressed to the front and actually took command of the American forces. Led by Arnold, the Continentals turned a near defeat into a resounding victory. Burgoyne, surrounded, defeated and with no hope of aid from other British forces, was compelled to surrender on October 17, 1777. There is a very strong tradition regarding the Battle of Saratoga that leads to the belief that two cannons and a number of British prisoners were taken to Pawtuxet.

THE BATTLE OF RHODE ISLAND

The great American victory at Saratoga, plus the eloquence and persuasive powers of Benjamin Franklin, brought about the long desired Franco-American alliance against the British. When in 1778 it became obvious that a large French fleet would be sent to America, Rhode Island's hopes were high that the British could be driven from Aquidneck Island.

Word reached Warwick that the date set for the invasion of Aquidneck Island was August 12. Unfortunately, one of the area's most devastating hurricanes wreaked havoc at that time on American and French strategies. The storm struck the American troops on Aquidneck Island on the evening of August 11, 1778. It tore up tents and leveled the American camp on the island, filling trenches, destroying stores and soaking powder and cartridges to uselessness. Without protection from the wind and rain, the men found sleep impossible. Lacking dry ammunition, the Americans' situation was desperate. Despite these setbacks, Sullivan, at 6:00 a.m. on August 15, ordered the American army to move south.

After careful consideration, the decision was made to fall back to the fortifications near Butt's Hill on the north end of Aquidneck Island. On August 28, the American army began its strategic retreat, with Nathanael Greene leading the troops from the trenches near the British lines. Many residents along Warwick's coast went to high hills to try to see what was happening. According to Horace Belcher, "Polly Rhodes, watching through a spy glass from an upper window of a Rhodes house on the Warwick side of Main St. in Pawtuxet saw the dark clouds of smoke hovering over the waters of the lower bay." Her husband, Sylvester Rhodes, and many of her friends and neighbors of the Pawtuxet Rangers were engaged in this classic battle.

It was during this action that Colonel Greene's Black Regiment, under Major Samuel Ward Jr., won everlasting fame. The ex-slaves repulsed three Hessian attacks. This was accomplished with some of the most fierce hand-to-hand combat of the entire war, as the American troops, many of them armed only with knives, repulsed the Hessian bayonet charges. Within a short time, as the militia units returned to Pawtuxet and Warwick from their heroic efforts in the Battle of Rhode Island, their feeling of accomplishment was great. They agreed with Lafayette's comment that "this was the best fought action of the war," but the fact remained that it was not a great and total victory.

In Pawtuxet, the economic crisis worsened in 1778. Self-serving speculators, styled in the eighteenth century as "engrossers and forestallers," were buying all necessary articles, especially food and clothing, for private gain. Over two thousand persons had been driven from Aquidneck Island as a result of the British action there. They were "homeless and penniless," dependent on what little public and private charity was available. Pawtuxet, already suffering, found little hope in caring for those who made their way to the town. The British finally evacuated Newport on October 25, 1779, and on October 18, 1781, Lord Cornwallis, British commander at Yorktown, Virginia, surrendered his entire eight-thousand-man army to the American and French troops. While it is true that the Battle of Yorktown was a deciding factor in ending the Revolutionary War, it did not mark the end of the suffering for Warwick and Rhode Island—the war lingered on until April 1783.

The "Otherwise Minded"

It was soon obvious that the state's soldiers had returned home not only with their health impaired, but with empty pockets as well. The Continental, or paper, money issued by Congress was considered totally unsatisfactory. Soon the phrase "not worth a Continental" began to be used to show worthlessness and contempt.

Because of the difficulties arising from war debts, Rhode Island soon found itself at odds with its sister states over raising revenue to support the federal government, which was facing serious financial difficulty. Congress asked for the power "to lay a duty of five per cent…on all goods, with certain exceptions, imported after May 1, 1781." Eventually, twelve states agreed, but Rhode Island refused, causing a crisis so severe that it eventually forced the abandonment of the Articles of Confederation as a form of government and brought about the necessity of drafting a new constitution. The arguments and discord in Rhode Island raged on from 1782 to 1790, with eventual disruption along political lines within the state nearly causing a rebellion. It was not until May 1790 that Rhode Island eventually joined its sister states in ratification of the Constitution.

The ratification brought increased prosperity to Warwick, especially to the seacoast village of Pawtuxet. Much of this was due to the fact that shortly after Rhode Island became the thirteenth state, Congress passed an act on June 14, 1790, establishing two ports, Pawtuxet and Bristol, for the districts of Providence and Newport, respectively, as "ports of entry" or "ports of delivery." In addition, there was a flourishing shipyard located just below the mouth of Pawtuxet Cove on the Warwick side, where, according to local historians, the firm of Brown & Francis had its ship, *Sally*. Pawtuxet historian Horace Belcher points out that in order to provide the large quantity of

Much of the charm of this lovely village can be found along Post Road. Many of the houses remain much as they were in 1924, when this photo was taken. *Warwick Historical Society Collection.*

rope used in the sailing industry, there was a ropewalk at "the Post Road end of present South Atlantic Avenue, in the rear of the Carr house…and extending past North Fair St."

The decade following the adoption of the Constitution by Rhode Island was exciting and promising for the seacoast towns. While Warwick was not directly involved in the East Indies trade, the ports of Pawtuxet and Apponaug benefited from the increased activity in Providence. The Jeffersonian embargoes of 1805–07 and the War of 1812 dealt the maritime trade a severe blow. By that time, however, some of the profits of the China trade and from the increased trading activity along the coast were already being diverted to the fledgling textile industry introduced to Rhode Island by Moses Brown and Samuel Slater.

Prosperity

On October 3, 1794, shortly after Samuel Slater and Moses Brown demonstrated that textiles could be successfully produced in America, a company was organized to manufacture cotton by machinery at the Centerville village in Warwick. Shortly after the mill was established, the Rhodes family in Pawtuxet became interested in the new industry. Robert

Rhodes and his sons had been very successful in the "coastal trade" and, by the turn of the century, expanded into other areas. Starting with a small gable-roofed mill, built south of the Pawtuxet Bridge, Christopher and William Rhodes made their successful entry into the textile industry. These brothers formed the C&W Rhodes Manufacturing Company and, in 1810, built a three-story mill on the northwest side of the bridge. This company was one of the first to manufacture broadcloth, and O.P. Fuller tells us that this venture "succeeded so well that the brothers extended their business to Natick."

Christopher and William Rhodes of Pawtuxet were quick to realize the advantages of a road that would connect their textile mills to Providence and New London. The Rhodes brothers and several others obtained a charter in 1816 to establish a toll road, which was later called the New London Turnpike. By 1821, the road was completed and stagecoaches were operating on a regular schedule.

Christopher Rhodes

One of the most influential of all politicians in the early nineteenth century was Christopher Rhodes, who lived in an imposing and beautiful home at 25 Post Road in the Pawtuxet section of Warwick. In addition to his early textile mills, a great deal of the success of Christopher Rhodes was due to his ability to recognize the need for adequate financing and cooperation among industrialists.

Christopher Rhodes's active political life spanned a time period of over half a century. From 1828 to 1831, he was the state representative for the town of Warwick and became well known for his strong stand on prison reform and on abolishing the whipping post and pillory as forms of punishment. As a result, he was appointed to the building committee for the erection of a state prison, which stood at the northwest side of the cove in Providence until it was razed in 1921.

A crisis arose in the 1830s on a social and fraternal aspect of village life when the Freemasonry movement was seriously jeopardized. The threat seriously affected the lives of a number of Pawtuxet's prominent citizens who were members of Harmony Lodge #9, which met at the Bank Café. At the height of the anti-Masonic hysteria, the Rhode Island General Assembly asked the Masons to discontinue and revoked the civil charters that had been granted to the lodges. In Pawtuxet, the Harmony Lodge went underground, and members met secretly at the Christopher Rhodes

The state fair in Pawtuxet was promoted by the Rhodes family. It brought merchants, businessmen, artisans and farmers together to bolster the economy. Since then, the building has served a variety of purposes. *Warwick Historical Society Collection.*

House. By 1842, the Dorr Rebellion turned Rhode Island's attention away from the anti-Masonic movement, and within a year, the Masons were able to resume their meetings.

THE CIVIL WAR

The American Civil War (1861–1865) marked a very definite turning point in Warwick's history. Many young men from the town's oldest families once again went to war. Fuller's history of the town lists at least fifteen Arnolds and six Rhodes men from Pawtuxet. Among the most famous Pawtuxet heroes was Elisha Hunt Rhodes, whose diary and letters of the Civil War have been published in the late twentieth century as a bestselling memoir, *All for the Union*, and have been featured in the PBS-TV series *The Civil War*. His letters offer insight into the struggle that is unequaled.

Warwick's Powerful Politicians

Rhodes's political influence extended beyond his official capacities to his business acquaintances and his family members. The house at 25 Post Road was the scene of the marriage of Christopher's daughter Eliza to John R. Bartlett and of his daughter Sarah to Henry B. Anthony. Both sons-in-law became very powerful political entities and played key roles in the state's development.

John Russell Bartlett had earned a reputation as a leading writer and politician by the mid-nineteenth century. He was the Rhode Island secretary of state from 1855 to 1872. Among his most noteworthy accomplishments was that he helped create the boundaries for the state of Arizona and was primarily responsible for the establishment of the Providence Athenaeum.

During the Civil War, Bartlett was acting governor from 1861 to 1862, while Governor Sprague took leave to command the Rhode Island troops encamped in Washington and in the First Battle of Bull Run. While serving as Rhode Island secretary of state, Bartlett became deeply interested in the history of Rhode Island. For ten years, Bartlett occupied himself in arranging and editing the state records. The result of this work is the ten-volume reference classic *Records of the Colony of Rhode Island and Providence Plantations*.

Christopher Rhodes's daughter Sarah Aborn Rhodes married Henry Bowen Anthony on October 16, 1838. Like Christopher Rhodes's other son-in-law, Anthony had a brilliant career in literature and politics. After being a frequent contributor to, and editor of, the *Providence Journal*, Anthony became a joint owner of the paper in 1840. Henry B. Anthony was elected governor on the Whig ticket in 1849 and again in 1850. In 1859, he was selected as a U.S. senator and remained in that capacity until his death in 1884. Anthony was skilled at using the shortcomings of the Rhode Island Constitution to control the state. With the help of Charles Brayton, Anthony was, for many years, the "political boss" of Rhode Island.

The Trolley

One significant impetus to the shore resort trade in the early part of the twentieth century was the development of the trolley system in Warwick. During the nineteenth century, public transportation was confined primarily to horse-drawn vehicles of the Union Railroad, which had been established by Amasa and William Sprague in 1865.

During the early twentieth century, this trolley could be seen speeding across the bridge through Pawtuxet. *Madeline Toy Collection (WHS).*

When the Sprague textile empire collapsed in 1873, a group of stockholders headed by Jesse Metcalf, prominent Providence businessman and part owner of the *Providence Journal*, purchased the Sprague horsecar trolley enterprise. Metcalf led the way for a drive to electrify the horsecar railway and was successful by 1892, when the first electric trolley was operating in Providence. The electric trolley captured the imagination and support of Rhode Islanders, as the new system proved faster and quieter than the horse-drawn railroad, and it was cheaper, cleaner and more efficient than the steam locomotives.

By the end of the first decade of the twentieth century, trolley lines ran from Providence through all of eastern Warwick. In time, the automobile and bus brought about an end to the trolley car. By the 1930s, streetcar companies found that the long lines to the suburbs were not economically feasible, and the streetcars were operated only on an intracity basis in Providence.

EARLY FIREFIGHTERS

One of the most serious hazards that plagued Pawtuxet in the early twentieth century was fire. From 1891 until the formation of the Warwick Firemen's League in 1926, major fires in the town brought about the creation of a

The pride of the village in the late nineteenth and early twentieth centuries was in the victories of the fire company's pumping prowess. The Fire King Fife & Drum Corps made each event even more festive. *Warwick Historical Society.*

number of fire departments. In 1891, after a very serious blaze destroyed a large part of the Cranston section of Pawtuxet Village, Volunteer Fire Company No. 1, Pawtuxet, was incorporated and purchased a hand engine called "Fire King." Within a year, the hand engine and the new company gained fame and made the cause for fire companies more popular when it played a key role in a Pawtuxet fire that threatened to destroy the village. Fighting that blaze, the volunteers quickly dropped the engine's suction pump into one of the deepest areas at the Cranston side of the Pawtuxet River dam and soon had a steady stream playing on the burning buildings.

In the first two decades of the twentieth century, there were still many more horses and carriages than there were automobiles in the village, but the trend toward the motor car was sure and steady. The first automobile in the area arrived in 1898 and was a steam-powered car. By 1901, an electric "truck" was already making deliveries in Providence, and by 1920, the gasoline-powered automobile was here to stay. From fewer than eight hundred automobiles registered in Rhode Island in 1900, the number had grown to well over forty thousand by 1920. This meant an increased popularity of Warwick as a resort area, and as a result, the village of Pawtuxet grew as a suburban entity.

During World War I, Pawtuxet residents had high hopes for a much better world and hoped this was truly "the war to end all wars." Unfortunately, the enthusiasm and patriotism once felt by Rhode Islanders turned to bitter cynicism by the 1920s. The poor foreign policies of President Warren G. Harding's administration, coupled with the failure of Rhode Island manufacturers to improve and update their holdings, saw the beginning of the end to the once predominant textile industry along the Pawtuxet River.

In addition to the decline in the textile industry, many residents were stunned by the passage of the Eighteenth Amendment in January 1919, which prohibited "the manufacture, sale or transportation" of intoxicating beverages. There was disbelief, disappointment and a sense of being deprived of a liberty of conscience and free will. Warwick never did become "dry" in reality, and it would appear that if all 1,520 federal agents hired to enforce the Volstead Act were stationed in the Pawtuxet Valley, the flow of liquor would still have continued uninhibited. Warwick, like many other cities and towns in Rhode Island, became infamous for smuggling and bootlegging. In addition, Warwick, with its many speakeasies in Oakland Beach, Pawtuxet and Apponaug, gained the reputation of being a "wide-open" town.

Pawtuxet, like the rest of the area, weathered the Great Depression and the Hurricane of 1938, World War II and Hurricane Carol. During the

The Bank Café has been one of Pawtuxet's most familiar landmarks since the period following the Civil War. *Horace Belcher Collection (WHS).*

postwar years, Pawtuxet villagers began to take great pride in their historic past. Thanks to the foresight of a number of residents, some of the state's most historic residences have been preserved amid tasteful commercial enterprises, blending the past and the present to the delight of all who live and visit here.

In addition to the charm of its winding streets and old houses, Pawtuxet Park offers lovely vistas, and the annual Gaspee Days not only reminds us of the first armed conflict of the Revolutionary War, but also offers a great parade along lovely Narragansett Parkway and a chance for local artisans to show their wares.

All in all, Pawtuxet Village, one of the oldest in New England, is a treasure in this modern age.

Pontiac

On Oct. 4, 1850, Mr. Clark sold out the estate to Zachariah Parker and Robert Knight for $40,000. In 1852, the premises passed into the hands of the present owners, the Messrs. B.B. & R. Knight, who changed the name of the place to Pontiac. Various changes have been made in the mills, as well as in the general appearance of the village since it has been in possession of the Knights.
—*Oliver Payson Fuller,* History of Warwick, *1875*

Warwick, a modern and dynamic city, is constantly growing and changing. Fortunately, in the last few decades, while changes have been inevitable to keep pace with modern needs and wants, enough concerned citizens and leaders have taken pains to ensure that the city's heritage is not forgotten. This is especially true in Pontiac, where the effort to keep the historic fabric of the village is alive and well. Now, in the first decade of the twenty-first century, the village of Pontiac is undergoing a great deal of new development. In addition to the modern shopping malls that have made Warwick a leading retail center in Rhode Island, we have seen the construction of a modern 163-room hotel on the site of the historic Pontiac Mill. The mill has long been a landmark in Warwick that reminds us of the time when the Fruit of the Loom textiles were the most famous in the world and when immigrants from England, Sweden, French Canada and Italy came to Pontiac village to find work and a new way of life. Pontiac, while having a number of unique features, is an excellent example of the mill villages that abounded in Rhode Island.

Oliver Payson Fuller, in his 1875 *History of Warwick*, notes, "Not one of the villages on the Pawtuxet River and its tributaries has been designated by

This fine drawing, found in Oliver Payson Fuller's 1875 history of Warwick, shows the earliest mill. Not long after, it was replaced by the handsome brick structure that stands today.

BLEACHERY
T. SHUELER SC
HERY, WARWICK, R. I.

so many different names in the course of its history, as the one we have now come to." He traces the names back to May 10, 1662, when Warwick records show that it was known by the Indian name of *Toskeunk*. Fuller, commenting on the Indian names for the area, says that the English settlers in Warwick found the Indian names difficult. As was their custom, they renamed the village, calling it "the Great Weir," as many fish, including salmon, shad and herring, migrated here and were caught with "weirs" or water traps.

The story goes on to say that later, when a bridge was built across the river, the people rechristened the place as the "Great Bridge Near the Weir." The man most closely identified with the bridge was Captain Benjamin Greene, also known as "Tobacco Ben Greene," as he raised large quantities of tobacco. For a number of years, the area was called Captain Benjamin Greene's Bridge. Captain Benjamin Greene gave his land and homestead to his grandson, Benjamin Arnold, and the bridge eventually was called Arnold's Bridge.

The Arnolds erected a saw- and gristmill along the river in 1810. For a while they prospered, but in 1829 the Arnolds ran into difficulty and sold the mills. In 1830, John H. Clark purchased the land at auction and bought the remaining mills still owned by the Arnolds. Clark was very successful, and within a few years the village of Arnold's Bridge was more often called Clarksville. In 1832, Clark built a stone factory for weaving, and in 1834, he constructed a large bleachery. O.P. Fuller credits Clark with bringing the name Pontiac to the village. He explained that Pontiac was the name of a celebrated Indian chief. Clark saw a picture of Pontiac, had it engraved and used it as a label on his goods.

THE B.B. & R. KNIGHT COMPANY

In 1850, Clark decided to sell his interests in the area. The mills were purchased by Zachariah Parker and Robert Knight for $40,000. Parker soon wanted to sell his interest, and Robert Knight contacted his brother, Benjamin Brayton Knight, and offered him a partnership. This was the beginning of the B.B. & R. Knight Company, which dominated the textile industry in Rhode Island for over fifty years. The man most responsible for the success of the Knight Company was Robert Knight. His was the classic American story of a poor boy who worked hard and became rich. From humble beginnings on a small farm, by 1886 he had acquired a fortune estimated at $50 million.

By 1858, the Knights had enlarged the bleachery, and when the old building burned down they replaced it with a stone building with over three

The Pontiac Bleachery and Mill became world famous by the late nineteenth century. The Fruit of the Loom label was a guarantee of quality. *Bob Byrnes Collection.*

times the capacity of the old. In 1863, they tore down the old stone mill and replaced it with a handsome new brick mill. The success of the Knights was phenomenal. When the A. & W. Sprague textile empire collapsed after the Panic of 1873, the Knights were in a position to purchase many of the Sprague mills. In a relatively short time, the firm of B.B. & R. Knight was able to use its great business skill to forge an even greater textile company than that enjoyed by the Spragues. In 1883, the financial success of the Pontiac Mill enabled the Knights to purchase the four Natick mills for $200,000 from the Union Company, which represented the creditors of the Spragues. In the following year, the Knights bought the Spragues' Arctic Mill, one of the finest in the state, for $175,000. Their success continued to be phenomenal. By the time of the Columbian Exposition of 1893, the firm was described as "one corporation, the largest in the world, [which] renders its dozen villages musical with the hum of 421,000 spindles and makes them beautiful by the happiness of more than 7,000 operatives."

Paternalism

Sociologists of the twentieth century have questioned the happiness of millworkers who were often rigidly controlled by the system, not only economically, but socially, morally and politically as well. While the Knights were "paternalistic mill owners" in every sense of the phrase, they did allow the workers more choices in Pontiac than was common in most comparable Rhode Island villages. As in other mill villages in the Pawtuxet Valley, however, Pontiac workers lived in houses built for them by the Knights, paid rent to the company and often shopped in the company stores for food raised on the company farms.

In 1866, additional tenements were built to house the increasing number of workers at the mill. Many of these well-constructed, one-and-a-half-story, gable-roofed buildings were designed by Clifton A. Hall, a well-known Providence architect. The Knights, like many other well-intentioned mill owners, believed that not only the physical but also the moral and religious well-being of the workers depended on them, and they sought to lead the way in the denomination that they deemed most appropriate. This was not always the choice of the workers, and as time has shown, this became more obvious.

At the turn of the century, the Knights owned nearly every building of significance in the village, including 120 of the 170 tenements. In addition to the four-story, 66- by 200-foot brick factory building, the company had a 40- by 160-foot bleachery, a large brick store and a storehouse of stone. The Knights' paternalism toward the fifteen hundred employees in the village went beyond providing a living for the worker and his family to caring for the intellectual and spiritual needs of the village. This was done by supporting the Pontiac Library and the All Saints' Episcopal Church.

THE ALL SAINTS' CHURCH

The church was organized in the spring of 1869, when Stephen N. Bourne, the mill superintendent, and fourteen interested Episcopalians met and elected officers. The Knight family immediately allowed the new parish to meet in the upper story of the company store and also provided a dwelling for the rector—both the dwelling and the hall were rent free. In addition, the Knights gave liberally toward paying the minister's salary. A few of the more influential ministers were the Reverend E.H. Porter, the first rector; Reverend William H. Williams; Reverend Laurence B. Thomas, who helped start the library; and the Reverend Edmund S. Rousmaniere, an excellent historian who was rector when the new church was built in 1888. In addition to the work at the church, the Reverend Rousmaniere's writings on the Pawtuxet villages have provided a great deal of insight toward understanding the role

All Saints' Church is one of the most beautiful edifices designed by the famous architect Howard Hoppin. *Warwick Historical Society Collection.*

played by the Greene and Brown families in the development of Rhode Island in the early years.

The church and parish house were the work of the distinguished Providence architect Howard Hoppin. The church membership included the more affluent families in Pontiac, as well as most of the English millworkers. The influence of the Knight family on the community was evident, as a special train brought two hundred people from Boston and Providence to take part in the dedication of the church.

Because of the Knights' generous contribution, the church was not only able to commission the architect Howard Hoppin, but it could also include many striking features that would have been too costly for the congregation. The Knights, for example, were responsible for five beautiful stained-glass windows. The central window, which contains the figure of a woman "in rich coloring and graceful drapery," was given in memory of Robert Knight's mother, while the two smaller windows on either side were in memory of his children. The Knight family worshipped here on a regular basis, and many parishioners came to see the family and to be seen by them.

All Saints' Church was one of the few nineteenth-century churches that did not charge a pew rental. The custom of the time and the necessity to raise funds made this a common practice. All Saints' was the exception, as this rent-free pew system was possible because the lion's share of the church's expenses was paid by the Knights. This included a portion of the clergy's salary as well.

For those who were not of the same faith, the Knights made other provisions. They provided room on the third floor of the company store for a school and allowed various buildings to be used as dance halls, a men's club and a library.

The Pontiac Library

The Knight family contributed heavily to the formation of the Pontiac Library. This was another one of the many ways in which the paternalism practiced by the influential and affluent Knights made its impact on the village. Like so many other "gifts" of the mill owners, it was appreciated by the villagers at the time, and today modern villagers continue to benefit from the generosity of the Knights in this area.

The Pontiac Free Library Association began on September 18, 1884, primarily through the efforts of the rector of All Saints' Church, Reverend Laurence B. Thomas. Reverend Thomas received a great deal of support and assistance from David Alexander, the superintendent of the Pontiac Mill. Alexander, with the consent of the mill owners, arranged for the library association to use a one-room schoolhouse on Knight Street. This first library building, according to a brief history compiled in 1984, had a potbellied stove, woven straw rugs and lamps hanging from a curved ceiling. Most importantly, it had over six hundred volumes and the interest of the Knight family.

One of the earliest active participants in library work was Miss Edith Knight, who served as librarian from 1912 to 1914 and again from 1915 until 1917. Miss Adelaide Knight and Mrs. Sophie Knight Rousmaniere were also active in library work and generous in both time and money. From the very beginning, the library was very successful in raising funds through "entertainments, suppers, and concerts." In 1932, the library moved to the renovated Thomas Byrne store on Greenwich Avenue. It remained there until 1957, when the present-day brick structure was built. Most residents of Pontiac associate the library with Jane A. Johnson, who was librarian from 1924 until 1966. The Pontiac Free Library has succeeded in providing modern services without abandoning the special qualities that marked libraries of the late nineteenth and early twentieth centuries.

It was not all work and no play in Pontiac Village. All were treated to summer concerts by a very talented group of musicians. *Millie Longo Collection (WHS).*

Immigration

During the latter part of the nineteenth century, the Pontiac Mill continued to prosper. This, however, had a very significant impact on the village. During this period, changes came about in the ethnic makeup of the village and the increased paternalism on the part of the Knights. Before the nineteenth century ended, however, the new immigrants who came to work in the mills were beginning to exhibit an independent spirit and brought their own values and identities to the village.

The first mill hands at the Pontiac Mill were from surrounding farms, but soon it was obvious that more workers were needed. During the 1860s, large numbers immigrated to Pontiac from the heavily industrialized areas of England. Many were from Lancashire and were accustomed to the paternalistic mill villages there. As they had in England, most British immigrants worked at the mill, lived in mill houses, read the mill newspaper, traded in the mill company store and attended Episcopal church services arranged by the mill owners.

Due to harsh economic conditions in Ireland and eastern Canada, many Irish and French-Canadians found work in the Knight-owned mills, and many found their way to Pontiac. Most of these immigrants were Catholic and found their churches in nearby Apponaug or Natick.

As the expansion of the mills brought about the need for more labor in the early 1870s, workers from Sweden came to Pontiac in large numbers and made a very dramatic impact on the village. As might be expected, most of those immigrants came to work at the mill and lived in company housing. In time, however, the Swedish immigrants built their own houses, traded frequently at C.A. Johnson's grocery store and wanted churches of their own denominations. Many of the houses along King Street and Reed Street are excellent examples of the fine dwellings built by these immigrants.

While they at first lived in company houses, shopped in the company store and sent their children to the company school, there were some aspects of life in Pontiac Village that they sought to change. Relatively soon after these immigrants began to arrive, the desire for a Swedish church made itself known. The first services of the newly organized congregation were held in a small Adventist church on Greenwich Avenue, on about the same ground as the present church.

The first pastor of the Evangelical Lutheran Church was the Reverend T.O. Linell of Topeka, Kansas. The church was still small and had to share the expenses of the pastor's salary, which was $800 a year, with congregations in Providence and Rumford. As a result, the Reverend Linell preached at Pontiac only on every other Sunday. The mill owners in Pontiac took an interest and helped support the church. We are told that "Mr. Webster Knight provided Rev. Linell with a dwelling and gave one hundred dollars yearly toward his salary as long as he stayed with the congregation." The number of workers arriving from Sweden grew, and soon the small church was no longer able to contain the congregation. Once again, the mill owners stepped in. "Messrs. Benjamin and Webster Knight…were friendly to the Swedes and their church. They donated a tract of land for a church and cemetery and deeded it on March 30, 1876." Soon after, a church fifty feet long and thirty feet wide was erected.

Some of the funds to support the church came from membership dues. In those days, the membership dues were fifty cents per month for each member who lived within twelve miles of the church and twenty-five cents for those who lived farther away. This system continued until 1924, when it was decided that each member should contribute according to his ability rather than pay fixed dues.

Shortly after Reverend Linell retired and Reverend Gottfrid Lundberg succeeded as pastor, a parsonage was built. The spirit of the times was reflected in the building of the church and house in several ways. It is said that Claes Ahlstrom sold his cow in order to buy a bell for the church. Those parishioners who were willing to help dig out the cellar received ten

St. Paul's Evangelical Lutheran Church, high on the hill overlooking Pontiac, is a wonderful visual reminder of the village's heritage and a credit to the community now, as it was then.

cents per hour for their labor. Before long, we are told, the building was ready for occupation.

The Reverend Abel Ahlquist had become the pastor in March 1914, and the church seemed destined for peace and tranquility. Nine months later, a fire, probably caused by faulty wiring, set the church ablaze. Reverend Ahlquist led his congregation in prayer as they gathered near the smoking ruin that once was their church. The Reverend Ahlquist made an eloquent plea for rebuilding the church and almost at once work was begun. By September 1916, the new church was completed and ready for use.

Donations were gathered through a plan by which each member over eighteen years of age gave ten cents per week, and church organizations contributed as well. The simple, semi Gothic–type church was built by the Kingston Building Firm of Providence. When this frame structure was built, it had a seating capacity of about 350. The white building features a belfry with a large bell and a spire, crowned with a gilded Celtic cross. This new church was formally dedicated on May 20, 1917. When the new St. Paul Evangelical Lutheran Church was dedicated, the entire village celebrated, never realizing that within the next few years major changes would take place that would transform Pontiac and change the lives of many who lived there.

WORLD WAR I

In 1917, the United States entered World War I and nothing was ever the same again. Like those in other communities in the state, Pontiac residents bought war bonds, staged patriotic parades and in general took part in the patriotic zeal to make this "the war to end all wars" and to "make the world safe for democracy." While Warwick's young men were serving in Europe, the textile industry boomed in Pontiac, Apponaug and Natick as war contracts brought the factories in the Pawtuxet Valley to full production. The average weekly take-home pay for textile workers at the end of the war was fourteen dollars. Not all workers received the same wages, however. Those with skills received handsome salaries, and often discrimination played a role in the awarding of salaries. At the beginning of the 1920s, both churches and village enterprises fared well.

The Knights, enjoying the prosperity brought about by the war, responded generously in helping the churches on a number of occasions. In 1915, Webster and Prescott Knight had promised a tract of land adjacent to the church to the congregations of Natick and Pontiac to be used as a burial ground. In 1920, they donated $2,000 toward the

Many later workers wanted food from their native lands and the camaraderie of fellow immigrants. They found both in this mom and pop store. *Millie Longo Collection (WHS).*

construction costs of additions and improvements. In 1921, a cemetery was dedicated. It was called the Swedish Lutheran Cemetery and later the St. Paul Lutheran Cemetery.

While the many villagers rejoiced in their bounty, it was becoming obvious that very little in Pontiac was the same after World War I ended. Veterans returned home disillusioned and cynical. Women received the right to vote in the state in 1917, and in 1919, the Prohibition Amendment was introduced. Warwick, which had long sponsored temperance movements, was now divided, as large numbers of immigrant workers in the mill villages opposed the concept. Pontiac, like many other areas of Warwick, had its share of speakeasies and bootleggers. While Pontiac was attempting to adjust to the changes, adverse conditions battered the area. In 1918–19, a very severe winter in which trolley lines were tied up and people were isolated was followed by an influenza epidemic that especially affected those in the mill villages.

The Long and Terrible Strike of 1922

Everyone in Pontiac was shocked and disturbed when it was learned that the Knights had sold their firm to the Consolidated Textile Corporation of New York. The era of paternalism was rapidly coming to a close, and in January 1922 the small Warwick village of Pontiac was drastically upset by one of the area's most devastating strikes, which resulted in an eight-month walkout by mill hands. Before it ended, there was widespread turmoil and suffering throughout the Pawtuxet Valley. Mills closed, nearly five thousand workers were idle, bread lines formed, armed soldiers patrolled the villages and nearly all business activity ceased. The villagers in Pontiac soon found that the prosperous period that followed World War I was over.

The paternalistic rule of Robert Knight and his son Webster ended when Webster Knight and his brother, C. Prescott Knight, sold their mills. The Consolidated Textile Corporation, the new owner, purchased the B.B. & R. Knight name and the Fruit of the Loom trademark, hoping to continue to enjoy high profits as the Knights had for so many decades. Almost immediately, however, Consolidated Textile found that this was not going to occur as it began to suffer losses because of a declining market and competition from the South and Europe. In 1921, to cut costs, the company lowered wages by 22.5 percent and increased the number of hours operatives were required to work per week. Millworkers in Pontiac grumbled but continued to work, with the hope that an increase in demand would bring prosperity to the mill owners and earlier pay cuts would be restored.

On January 20, 1922, these hopes were lost as news reached the village that the Goddard Brothers and the owners of the B.B. & R. Knight Company were going to cut wages an additional 20 to 22 percent. On January 21, 1922, 250 weavers at the Royal Mill in Riverpoint and workers in the Natick and Pontiac mills declared a strike. News of the walkout dominated the front page, even overshadowing the report of the death of Pope Benedict XV and of three cases of smallpox in Warwick. Shortly after this, over 3,000 strikers met at Vanesse Hall in Phenix with the objective of getting all millworkers in the valley to join in the strike. Within a short time, professional organizers James A. Dick and William Derrick entered Rhode Island. Dick assumed control and marched the strikers from Phenix to the Pontiac Bleachery to attempt to persuade the workers in the mills to walk out.

Violence was inevitable. Rioting erupted on January 31, 1922, at the nearby Natick mill, where a number of Pontiac residents worked. Police from Warwick, West Warwick and Coventry were called out to quell the disturbance, which began when an alleged rioter was arrested. The mob began smashing windows and throwing stones at the mill, and the situation was rapidly getting out of control. For the next few days, many in Pontiac and other mill villages in the Pawtuxet Valley lived under the shadow of violence and retaliation.

Without wages, workers were faced with severe economic repercussions. Those who lived in company houses were threatened with eviction, and many were with little or no food. In an attempt to help, the unions opened cafeterias to help feed the destitute. Hopes for an early settlement were dashed when workers asked for the restoration of wage cuts and a forty-eight-hour week and management refused on February 1. The mill owners believed that arbitration would solve nothing and demanded that the governor call out the troops. On February 20, 1922, Governor San Souci called out the National Guard. The strike that began on January 21, 1922, lasted for eight months and did irreparable damage to both the mills and the mill villages. When the strike finally came to an end, the paternalistic relationship of mill owners and workers had disintegrated, and the textile industry no longer ruled supreme in Rhode Island.

Very serious charges of police brutality and other crimes brought about more bitterness between the workers and government officials. Unfortunately, in many cases the extra constables added to the police forces were untrained and, at times, even more undisciplined than the rioters. On several occasions, union officials claimed that the strikebreakers brought about the very violence that they were there to suppress. Union leaders pointed out sadistic behavior on the part of both the strikebreakers and newly appointed constables, all to no avail.

San Souci, who had great optimism for a peaceful settlement at the beginning of the strike, was now stunned by the turn of events. Reluctantly, he bowed to the wishes of the mill owners and sent the mounted command of the National Guard to the villages of Pontiac and Natick. Over 150 troops, many of them on horseback, arrived at Brown Square in Natick to stop a riot at the mill during the last week of February 1922.

For a very short time, it appeared that Rhode Island would be faced with its most serious rebellion when over one thousand men, women and children gathered to face the troops. Many of these people were from Pontiac. A *Pawtuxet Valley Times* article relates that "Father Tirrocchi of St. Joseph's Church in Natick came running out of the rectory and pleaded with the crowd in Italian to go home and avoid bloodshed." His plea was heeded, and gradually, as cool heads prevailed, the crowd disappeared from the square.

By midsummer, both sides were weary of the strike and were getting desperate. Finally, on September 12, 1922, the mill owners agreed to restore the wage scale that had been in effect before January 1922. Looking back, many historians feel that this helped bring about the end of New England's supremacy in the textile industry. The conditions that had existed during the period in which the Knight family ruled the village as benevolent despots no longer existed. Pontiac residents looked to their own resources to find the strength to weather the severe economic depression that came in the 1930s.

GOOD AND BAD TIMES

For a time, it seemed that nothing would ever help the village get back on its feet. For the three decades that followed the Strike of 1922, Pontiac witnessed not only a severe economic depression, but a devastating hurricane and a major world war as well. In addition to the experiences shared with the entire state, many who lived in Pontiac have special memories that emphasize the unique relationships that existed between villagers and the mills, churches, schools and other villagers. All recollections of village life during the early twentieth century were not necessarily pleasant, as Pontiac residents had their share of tragedy and heartbreak and often wondered if the village would survive the decline of the textile industry.

Throughout the difficult times, however, there remained a strong sense of community as neighbors helped and consoled one another. While many of the close relationships were within ethnic lines, there was also a spirit that crossed the boundaries to ease the pain of the "bad" times and share the joy of the "good" times. All was not "gloom and doom." During the early twentieth century, the mill sponsored a men's club where operatives could go on Friday and Saturday nights to play cards and exchange experiences and ideas. For men, women and children, pleasant memories revolve around the summer concerts of the Pontiac Brass Band, which was founded by the villagers. The band played every Friday night and, along with the special programs at the school and library, gave Pontiac residents a much-needed respite from the pressures of life during the years of economic hardship.

Many of Pontiac's residents, looking back through the rose-colored glasses of nostalgia, recall with pleasure their days of growing up and living in the village during the early part of the twentieth century. While some of the older citizens remembered the long, hard hours at the mill, the low wages, crowded tenements, fear of economic depression and the closing of the mill, others recalled only the pleasant experiences.

Mrs. Hattie Anderson, interviewed in 1974 by Margie Bucheit for the *Warwick Beacon*, looked back at an age that moved slowly and seemed more enjoyable. She noted:

> *Before there were electric lights the lamplighter would come around with his lantern to light the street lamps in the village. The roads in Pontiac*

were dirt roads and the houses were well kept up with flowers and gardens. Clothes were different then; they hung from the shoulder in a loose chemise style. Children had one dress for one week, another for the next and a good one for Sunday.

Nearly all residents of the village remember with nostalgia the tolling of the mill bell. It rang out to signal the beginning of the workday, the lunch break, the end of the day and the time for the children to stop playing and return home. Not only did it ring out every hour, but it rang on special occasions as well. One of the best remembered is when the Pontiac Mill bell joined with the bells of all the churches to ring out the joy of the end of World War II.

The Pontiac Railroad Station

During the early twentieth century, a great deal of Pontiac's life revolved around the railroad station, which was built in 1882. The small, one-story structure occupied the northeast corner of Greenwich Avenue and Reed Street until 1964. It was moved at that time to 2245 Post Road, where it was used as a lounge at the former Great House restaurant. In 2007, it was

The Pontiac train station, once very instrumental to the village, has been returned to Pontiac, beautifully restored and dedicated, thanks to Millie Longo and members of the association. *Warwick Historical Society Collection.*

returned to Pontiac, restored to its original splendor and has been a major part of Pontiac's revitalization.

During the nineteenth and early twentieth centuries, when transportation was difficult, the railroad was very significant to Pontiac's mills and villagers. The railroad station at Pontiac was a stop on the Pawtuxet Valley Branch Railroad, a line that connected Pontiac to the New York, Providence and Boston Railroad at Auburn and to the Providence, Hartford and Fishkill Railroad at a junction north of Natick.

Nearly everyone who lived in the village during the pre–World War II era has special memories of the station and of Jack McCabe, the freight agent and postmaster at Pontiac. McCabe began his career early in the 1900s and continued it for half a century. For decades, one of the prime targets at Halloween was the outhouse at the station. Trying to turn the building over as their older brothers had done was the ambition of many a young teenager during those years.

McCabe knew everyone in the village and all knew him. One of his daughters, Monica, now Mrs. Francis O'Neill, recently noted, "I came from an all-girl family and whenever we went to our proms or got married all the neighbors turned out to see us off in all our finery!" As she recalled Pontiac, Mrs. O'Neill remarked, "Everyone shared in the joys and sorrows, the highs and lows of each other's lives."

One of Pontiac's most memorable events occurred in 1958. In that year, the McCabes and the O'Neills attracted national attention because of the peculiarities of the mayoral race in Warwick. John J. McCabe, the endorsed Democratic candidate, was opposed by his son-in-law, Francis J. O'Neill. McCabe had been granted leave from the railroad station in 1954 to become city clerk under Mayor Joseph Mills. When Mills decided against running for mayor in 1956, McCabe became the endorsed Democratic candidate. As the favorite candidate, McCabe felt confident in taking a very strong stand in favor of getting a sewage system for Warwick and adopting a modern zoning ordinance.

A confident McCabe was shocked when his son-in-law took a different stand and opposed him. The intensity of the struggle became apparent as O'Neill came within twenty-six votes of upsetting McCabe in the Democratic primary. The struggle and controversy between the followers of McCabe and O'Neill seriously weakened the Democratic Party. As a result, on November 6, 1956, McCabe was defeated by a relative newcomer in Warwick politics, Raymond E. Stone, a Republican.

The one Democratic politician who seemed to weather all Republican victories was Lambert Lind, longtime councilman from Ward Eight. Lind's commitment to Pontiac and Warwick's highway system has earned him the honor of having part of Route 5 called the Lambert Lind Highway. One of the favorite stories concerning Lind was recorded in 1958. Lind was thirty minutes late in arriving at the council meeting. The reason was that a constituent informed him of a large pothole at Central and Knight Streets in Pontiac. Lind decided that it needed immediate attention. According to the story, he "rolled a couple of good sized stones into the crater, got a shovel from his car, threw in gravel and then ran his car wheels 'steamroller fashion' over it until the road was fairly smooth."

Politics

Life in the mill villages differed from life on the farm, as most of the villagers were immigrants who worked at the mills. At first, differences among the ethnic groups kept them separated politically, as well as socially, but as early as the first decade of the twentieth century it became obvious that there was a common cause and that the residents of the mill villages differed from their neighbors in the agricultural sections of Warwick in areas other than language or occupation.

Political needs and ambitions were also apparent, as many of the newcomers had arrived after the Civil War and felt no loyalty to the Grand Old Party of Anthony, Brayton and Aldrich. Once the franchise was extended to the newcomers, discontent with the party bosses became apparent. For a period of time, ethnic differences kept them divided and impotent, but eventually the politically adept son of an Irish immigrant, Patrick Henry Quinn, succeeded in developing a potent political force. He convinced the leaders of the ethnic groups that their similarities were greater than their differences and allied them in the Democratic Party.

The Split

By 1909, the Democrats in the western section of Warwick, led by Quinn, gained control of the financial town meetings and broke the political control of the Old Guard in Warwick. The turmoil that resulted made it obvious that the needs and demands of the opposing elements could not be met with one government. After the death of Charles "Boss" Brayton, the demand for separation became greater, and petitions to the General Assembly were finally heeded.

On March 14, 1913, 8.3 square miles of territory, half the population and almost the entire industrial base of the town were separated. The third, fourth and fifth representative districts were chartered as the town of West Warwick. The transition was relatively smooth, as both towns saw the advantages of the move. While most of the mill villages were lost, Warwick still had the Elizabeth Mill in Hillsgrove, the Apponaug Company and the Pontiac Mill. These were, at the time, all thriving and valuable assets for the town.

A New Era Begins

The trolley line, which was established in 1910, made it much easier to commute to Providence and Cranston. New immigrants, some of whom worked in Warwick's mills and others who found it easier to live in Warwick, began to populate the area. Gradually, the close parochial sections of Pontiac began to broaden and become more cosmopolitan. World War I introduced Warwick and Rhode Island into a much larger world, and new problems arose that put the paternalistic mill villages as dominated by the B.B. & R. Knight Company at a disadvantage.

Prohibition and Speakeasies

During the early part of the century, the temperance movement seemed to have triumphed when the Eighteenth (or Prohibition) Amendment was passed in 1919. It soon became obvious, however, that the law was practically unenforceable. Warwick's small-town police force could do very little to stop the speakeasies that quickly came into existence. Many in Pontiac made their own beer, wine and other intoxicating beverages. Nearby Arctic and various sections of Warwick became notorious as "place[s] to get a drink." It has been said that as one of the illegal establishments was closed by the police, three others opened up to take its place.

Of a more threatening nature to most Pontiac residents was the beginning of an economic depression. The mills slowed down their production and jobs were scarce. With very little work being offered, the children in Pontiac, who earlier would have worked in the mills, stayed in school and began taking a greater interest in what was happening in areas beyond the village. Pontiac's young people were growing up in a world of rapid changes and were anxious to be part of the progress being made.

Pontiac

Becoming a City

Warwick's population in 1930 had risen to 23,196, giving rise to a general feeling that the town meeting form of government was no longer adequate. In 1931, Warwick became Rhode Island's eleventh city when its voters approved a charter for a mayor-council plan of city government. When Pierce Brereton took office as Warwick's first mayor, Warwick was still divided over whether to become a city or remain a small rural community. Pontiac, as Warwick's most clearly identified mill village, was torn by a desire to retain the advantages of the past and still enjoy the benefits of the late twentieth century. Merging two different eras was not an easy task, and Pontiac's mills, schools and churches were changed dramatically. Village pride suffered.

Warwick's first mayor, Republican Pierce Brereton, was succeeded by Democrat John O'Brien and, in 1936, by Republican Albert Ruerat, who held the office until 1948. Ruerat's long tenure witnessed the difficult process of uniting a number of nineteenth-century villages into a suburban city. While zoned for residential, farming, business and industrial districts, the increased migration to Warwick and other problems created by the Depression and the hurricane often turned well-intended plans into haphazard growth. This often resulted in the destruction of some of Warwick's finest attractions, to the detriment of villages such as Pontiac.

During most of the 1930s, villagers were preoccupied with economic conditions rather than efforts to preserve the historical fabric of the village. As there was less and less work at the Pontiac Mill, the search for employment became more acute, and rumors of hiring drew many of the later arrivals, such as the Italian immigrants, from Pontiac to Natick or Apponaug, where the mills were still operating. More often than not, the few jobs available were already taken and despair increased.

Families, to cut expenses, often shared housing, as they had done earlier in the century when the immigrants first arrived in the village. As a result, family units became even closer than they had been in the 1920s. Neighborhood stores, wherever possible, carried many of the villagers on credit, and a great deal of sharing of goods and hope for the future took place. While very few children in the section of Pontiac below the railroad tracks had bicycles, nearly all had some type of wagon that they could take to the mill dump in hopes of finding enough scrap metal or other junk to sell to the "rag man." While very few remember the horse and buggy or the grocery wagons, nearly all who lived through the 1930s can recall the "rag man." Another common memory was that of making beer. Long after Prohibition was repealed in 1933, economic hardships dictated that homemade beer

Today, most of the mill stands as it did in the nineteenth and twentieth centuries. The modern, state-of-the-art hotel on the site has been designed to blend with the old buildings.

and wine were still common beverages on many tables in Pontiac and the mill villages of Warwick and West Warwick.

All was not work with no play, however, as this was the time of great interest and active participation in sports of all types. During this period, baseball ruled supreme, and heated arguments over the relative merits of the Red Sox and Yankees could be heard in the mills, stores and schools in the area. Long before "little leagues" and organized sports, sandlot baseball, football and soccer were popular. Nearly everyone who lived in the village in the 1930s has some fond memories of the sports and games in the pre-television era when children were both seen and heard as they played in the streets and empty lots in the village.

The decade of the 1940s was again a time of many changes in Pontiac. By the end of that decade, village life centering on the mill was more of a memory than a fact. From 1941 until 1945, World War II remained prominent, and any major changes had to await the conclusion of hostilities and the return of the young men and women who served in the armed forces.

Mayor Ruerat, in later years, felt that one of the major contributions of his twelve years as mayor was to make Warwick "city conscious." He said in a 1986 interview for the *Warwick Beacon*, "When Warwick became a city, there were 19 separate villages. It took a lot of doing to get them to think not of their individual villages, but the city." Eventually, the combination of the experiences of Warwick's service people and the decline of the textile industry eliminated the predominant role of the paternalistic villages.

Despite efforts of the city administration, Pontiac still could not decide whether it wanted to become part of a full-fledged city or remain a small village. In many instances, residents sought to cling to the old concepts of villages, while on the other hand, they hoped to reap the benefits of city services. Pontiac continued, however, to take fierce pride in the accomplishments of its native residents, such as artist Mario Izzi, jewelry designer George Brickander and Roy F. Nelson, who rose from a poor family in Pontiac to an important position with the Texaco Company. In the period immediately following World War II, Pontiac went from a small, nearly self-sufficient village to become a part of the greater complex of the city of Warwick.

As the city grew in size, the Pontiac Mill, operated by the Fruit of the Loom company, continued to decline. In 1970, the Pontiac Mill finally stopped operating. The mill complex, consisting of twenty acres and thirty-four buildings, was purchased in June 1973 by the Migley Corporation owned by Henry Migliaccio. The mill, once the pride of the B.B. &

R. Knight Company, continued to serve in a practical way by providing inexpensive space for small businesses. The mill is recognized as an excellent visual reminder of the architecture and lifestyle of the nineteenth century in Pontiac Village, and the city and developers are aware of its value. Other late twentieth-century changes saw the once elegant Knight Farm on East Avenue becoming the Rhode Island Community College and malls coming into the area where there were once picturesque cow barns, pasturelands and undeveloped areas.

Pontiac Village today, thanks to the Village Association and awareness by the city administration, is very successful in maintaining its heritage and at the same time adapting to the needs of the twenty-first century. More than ever, a great deal of interest is shown in Pontiac in meeting twenty-first-century needs. More development along Route 5 is taking place, and very significant changes are happening at the old mill. The section that once housed bales of cotton and various other products has been demolished, and a large "boutique-style," 163-room hotel has been built on the site. In addition to the guest rooms or "lofts," the NYLO hotel also features a "living area" and a restaurant. Once this phase of building is totally completed, plans are being made for renovating the 1898 mill and redeveloping it for stores and condominiums.

All Saints' Church, St. Paul's Evangelical Lutheran Church and the Pontiac Library have preserved much of the area's charm, and the return of the Pontiac Railroad Station to the village has spurred new interest in the village. The station is a museum and, at the same time, a substation of the Warwick Police Department, keeping the old and the new in a pleasant and practical perspective. The past and future of Pontiac have been very well melded together.

About the Author

In 1985, Don D'Amato was appointed Warwick's first official city historian, a position he continues to hold today. Don's weekly column in the *Warwick Beacon*, those on the city's website and his numerous books have added a new dimension to the history of Warwick and Rhode Island. Many years of teaching history in the Warwick school system and at the Community College of Rhode Island have increased his knowledge and interest in the villages and heritage of the city. He has won statewide acclaim for his articles and books and is recognized as a positive force in the understanding of Rhode Island history. D[illegible] a graduate of Northeastern University (BA) and the University of [illegible] Island (MA). His many books include *Warwick's 350-Year Heritage*, [illegible] *Celebration*, *General James M. Varnum*, *Warwick Firefighters* and a hi[illegible] Johnson & Wales University.

The author at Pawtuxet Cove. *Photo by Paul Carey*[illegible]

Please visit us at
www.historypress.net